Revival Fire

150 YEARS OF REVIVALS

Spiritual Awakenings and Moves of the Holy Spirit
Days of Heaven on Earth!

Mathew Backholer

Revival Fire – 150 Years of Revivals, Spiritual Awakenings and Moves of the Holy Spirit – Days of Heaven on Earth!

Scripture quotations unless otherwise stated are taken from the Holy Bible, the New King James Version (NKJV). Published by Thomas Nelson, Inc. Copyright © 1982 by Thomas Nelson, Inc. Used by permission. All rights reserved.

References to deity are capitalised, whilst references to the evil one, the devil are not capitalised even though this is contrary to English grammar rules.

As is the nature of the internet, web pages can disappear and ownership of domain names can change hands. Those stated within the book were valid at the time of first publishing.

UK ISBN 978-1-907066-06-1

British Library Cataloguing In Publication Data
A Record of this Publication is available from the British Library

First Published in August 2007 under the title 150 Years of Revival – Revised and updated May 2010 by ByFaith Media

'For behold the Lord is coming out of His place; He will come down...The mountains will melt under Him, and the valleys will split like wax before the fire, like waters poured down a steep place' Micah 1:3-4.

- Jesus Christ is Lord -

Contents

Page

- Jesus Christ is Lord -

Revival Related Scriptures

- 'And it shall come to pass afterward that I will pour out My Spirit on all flesh. Your sons and your daughters shall prophesy, your old men shall dream dreams, your young men shall see visions; and also on My menservants and on My maidservants, I will pour out My Spirit in those days' Joel 2:28-29.
- Thus says the Lord, "For I will pour water on him who is thirsty, and floods on the dry ground; I will pour out My Spirit on your descendants, and My blessing on your offspring" Isaiah 44:3.
- Thus says the Lord, "Rain down, you heavens, from above, and let the skies pour down righteousness; let the earth be open, let them bring forth salvation, and let righteousness spring up together. I the Lord have created it" Isaiah 45:8.
- 'He shall come down like rain upon the mown grass, like showers that water the earth' Psalm 72:6.
- God said, "By those who come near Me, I must be regarded as holy; and before all the people I must be glorified" Leviticus 10:3.
- God said, "For My own sake, for My own sake, I will do it; for how should My name be profaned? And I will not give My glory to another" Isaiah 48:11.
- Thus says the Lord, "If My people who are called by My name will humble themselves and pray and seek My face and turn from their wicked ways, then I will hear from heaven, and will forgive their sin and heal their land" 2 Chronicles 7:14.
- 'Search me, O God, and know my heart; try me, and know my anxieties; and see if there is any wicked way in me, and lead me in the way everlasting' Psalm 139:23-24.
- 'The eyes of the Lord are on the righteous and His ears are open to their cry' Psalm 34:15.
- 'Turn away my eyes from looking at worthless things, and revive me in Your way' Psalm 119:37.
- 'O Lord, though our iniquities testify against us, do it for Your name's sake; for our backslidings are many, we have sinned against You' Jeremiah 14:7.

Prayer Meeting Revival (1857-1859)

3ᵉ American Awakening – N.Y. / million converted

The Prayer Meeting Revival is also known as the Fulton Street Revival, whilst some authors refer to it as the Second (or even Third) American Awakening. Though at the time it was known as the Great Revival because it swept across America, igniting 'at least 2,000' revivals which were in 'active progress' at the time of William C. Conant's collation in 1858 which was published under the title *Great Awakening of 1857-'8.*[1]

This move of God was noted for its fervent breadth of prayer and its worldwide influence which sparked revivals worldwide (see Appendix A) and was birthed from the Fulton Street Prayer Meeting, in New York City, America. Within the space of eighteen months (some say two years), one million people, became "born again" (as Jesus said in John 3), as they realised that Jesus Christ was the Saviour of the world, whilst another one million church members were set ablaze out of a population of thirty million! If a revival on that scale had broken out on the one hundred and fiftieth anniversary of the revival then ten million new converts across America would have been saved and ten million Church members would be on fire for the Lord!

On the first day of October 1856, the Holy Spirit began to 'especially manifest' at the Stanton Street Baptist Church, New York City; there was not a week when less than five or six persons presented themselves as inquirers to the Christian faith. During December 1856 to January 1857 'the interest increased' and by February, meetings were held every night. In March and April, sixty persons were baptised. During the summer there was a plateau and when 'the autumn and winter months came, the revival began anew, with increased fervour. In the space of eighteen months, about two hundred were baptised.'[2]

The autumn of 1857 was signalised by a sudden and fearful convulsion in the commercial world, as sources of prosperity dried up. 'On the 14 October 1857, the financial disorder which had prevailed with increasing severity for many weeks, reached its crisis in an overwhelming panic that prostrated the whole monetary system of the country, virtually in one hour' as the financial markets on Wall Street crashed.[3] Fred W. Hoffman wrote: 'Greedy speculation, excessive railroad development and a wild-cat currency system combined to bring about an unexpected collapse in the financial structure of the nation.

Hundreds of banks failed, specie payments were suspended, railroads went into bankruptcy and thousands of merchants and business houses were forced to close their doors. Factories were shut down...Stripped of their self-dependence and in despair, men again found time to think on their need of God."[4] Multitudes lost their jobs (there were 30,000 unemployed men in New York, alone) and masses of people tramped the streets with banners demanding bread. The nation was also divided (north and south) over the issue of slavery.

The Prayer Meeting Movement in New York started less than a month before the Wall Street crash, when lay missionary, Jeremiah C. Lamphier (who was greatly burdened for souls), began a weekly lunchtime prayer meeting for businessmen (though in time women joined the men). Most days, Lamphier would be found in prayer at the lecture room of the old North Dutch Church on the corner of Fulton Street and William Street, New York City.

Jeremiah Lamphier began his lay work in July 1857 and used to distribute tracts and visit families who lived in the vicinity of the church. In September he announced a weekly meeting to be held at noon, beginning on the 23 September 1857 which was publicised around the district. On the first day, after thirty minutes of praying alone he was joined by five people. The following week, twenty arrived and on the third week there were forty and then a hundred. It was at this third meeting that it was decided to begin daily lunchtime prayer meetings instead of weekly. Lots of people started to attend the prayer meetings, many were looking for better things, others searching for salvation whilst for some it was a means of killing time amongst their desperate, hopeless unemployment and inner turmoil. After four months, the Fulton Street hall grew too small so the meeting was moved to the largest hall in the city with seating capacity for four thousand!

By January 1858, there were 50,000 people in New York alone, who were praying at noon in one hundred prayer meetings across the city! Evening meetings in many churches were also commenced to further the work. The Burton's Theatre (which had formerly been a church), named after the English actor and playwright, had been idle for some time and was rented out for eighteen days, beginning on the 17 March 1857, as a place of prayer, worship and preaching, until the building passed into the hands of the United States government. Theodore Cuyler, Henry Ward Beecher and other men preached nightly and there were midday prayer meetings. The New York *Evening Post* reported on the last night that a religious meeting was held at the theatre, Henry Ward Beecher said, "What history has been here...God be thanked that heaven's gates have been opened in this place of hell."[5]

The story is told of a merchant who came to New York City to buy his goods. As the merchant was selecting his items he requested of the wholesaler to work through the noon hour, thus enabling him to return home by the usual boat. The merchant politely replied, "I cannot help that. I have something to attend to which is of more importance than selling goods. I must attend the noonday prayer meeting. It will close at one o'clock and I will fill out your order then." The visiting merchant was so impressed by this Christian's faithfulness, that on reflection he gave his life to the Lord. He returned to his home in Albany, New York and immediately started a noonday prayer meeting in the city.[6]

Prayers limited to 3-5 min

Prayer meetings were also begun in Philadelphia, Chicago and beyond. Many businessmen and workers would use their lunch hour to attend these prayer meetings which lasted exactly one hour. No person was permitted to openly pray for more than five minutes (in some meetings it was limited to three minutes) so that others present would have an opportunity. In other places, daily prayer meetings were held in the evenings. In New York, a hymn would be sung and then prayer would begin, along with prayer requests and testimonies of answered prayer. Prayer was for conversions, for their city, for help in honest dealing in business and for healing etc. Many merchants and businessmen got right with God and started to deal honestly, even debts of more than two decades old were repaid in full and those who had overcharged their customers made restitution. One merchant within New York told the people that 50,000 professed to be Christians within the city and the way to reach the 1,000,000 residents was to take an individual or family under one's special supervision and to lead them to Christ.[7]

For the first three days of December 1857, the Presbyterians held a conference at Pittsburgh. The theme was on revival, much of the time was spent in prayer and two hundred ministers and laymen attended. Those present were encouraged to instruct their congregations to pray for a spiritual awakening and a committee drew up an address which was to be read from the pulpits. On the first Sunday of the New Year (1858) the message was on the theme of revival, and the first Thursday was a day of prayer and fasting.[8]

In Canada, a supplement, containing information about the awakening from various American religious papers was printed in the Montreal *Witness*. It was widely circulated in Montreal and was given to every Protestant minister in Canada.[9]

During the winter of 1857-1858, the crime rate dropped, and under the circumstances of mass unemployment it could have been expected to rise as the destitute became desperate. However, the revival swept away many class barriers as the wealthy looked upon the under classes as their brothers and sisters in Christ and their physical needs were met, as well as their spiritual needs. This national revival was not remote piety in the corners of little churches, but at the fore of everyday business life, college life and home life. It was right there in the nitty-gritty of everyday work. It is worth noting that the lay influence predominated to such an extent that ministers were overshadowed and it very much became a lay revival with few recognised leaders, but holy men spoke as led by the Lord.

The New York dailies (newspapers) published several *Revival Extras* filled with accounts of the progress of the work in various parts of the land. Henry C. Fish in *Handbook of Revivals* (1874) wrote: 'The secular papers all spoke of it; and some of them made it a point to report the meetings fully' whilst 'the telegraph was called into requisition' – calling churches in other cities to pray, whilst individuals contacted their family to inform them of their conversions.[10]

In Pennsylvania, some lumbermen visited Philadelphia where Charles Finney was holding evangelistic meetings and they got converted. They returned home to their kinsfolk which was known as the lumber region and five thousand people were converted along an area of eighty miles and there was not a single minister of the Gospel there![11]

In 1859, on the second anniversary of the first noon prayer meeting a convention was assembled in Cooper Institute, New York City, to consider the means to sustain and enlarge the influence of the meetings. Representatives came from as far away as San Francisco. In Boston, a man stood up in one of the meetings and said, "I am from Omaha, Nebraska. On my journey east I have found a continuous prayer meeting. We call it about two thousand miles from Boston to Omaha, and here was a prayer meeting about two thousand miles in length."[12]

Charles Finney (who had been preaching at Boston at the beginning of the revival) stated 'that the winter of 1857-1858, will be remembered as a time when a great revival prevailed. It swept over the land with such power, that for a time it was estimated that no less than 50,000 conversions occurred weekly.' It was reported that in some towns of New England not a single person remained unconverted! People were converted inside and outside of church buildings – whilst going about their daily lives they would come under conviction of sin, at work or at home.

The *Methodist advocate* for January 1858 reported ten noteworthy features of the revival:
1. Few sermons were preached.
2. Lay brethren were eager to witness.
3. Seekers flocked to the altar.
4. Nearly every seeker had been blessed.
5. Experiences enjoyed remained clear.
6. Converts were filled with holy boldness.
7. Religion became a daytime social topic.
8. Family altars were strengthened.
9. Testimony given nightly was abundant.
10. Conversation was marked by a pervading seriousness.[13]

The battleship *North Carolina* with more than a thousand men onboard was anchored in New York Harbour. It was used as a naval receiving ship and so sailors were constantly coming and going after receiving their period of training and drafted to other ships. It was decided by four young Christian sailors from three different denominations to meet for united prayer. They were permitted to use the retired orlop deck which was situated far below the water line. During prayer, the Holy Spirit came and they burst forth into praise and worship. Sailors, upon hearing the young men began pouring below deck to mock and jeer, but came under deep and abiding conviction. Many remained to pray and cry for mercy; strong men were broken down. The meetings continued nightly, hundreds were converted and ministers on shore were sent for to assist in the work. John Shearer wrote: 'It was as if a vast cloud of blessing hovered over land and sea. Ships, as they drew near the American ports, came within a definite zone of heavenly influence. Ship after ship arrived with the same tale of sudden conviction and conversion…In one ship a captain and the entire crew of thirty men found Christ out at sea and entered the harbour rejoicing.'[14]

In Chicago, Dwight L. Moody was greatly affected by the revival. He left his very successful shoe business and went into fulltime Christian ministry. Over the next few decades, he went on to see phenomenal success on both sides of the Atlantic with his singing assistant, Ira Sankey. When Moody passed into glory in 1899, he left behind a legacy, his Bible Institute in Chicago, a girls school in Northfield, a boy's school at Mount Hermon and an estimated one million souls won through his ministry![15]

Dr. Thomas de Witt Talmage was known as the "Spurgeon of America" and counted senators, presidents and members of the European and Russian royal families as his friends. He saw revival in his parish at Belleville, New Jersey on the banks of the Passaic during the revival.[16]

This revival also launched a great American missionary movement, with missionaries going to India, China and Korea. Horace Underwood was a seminary student at the time. He went to Korea in 1885 (the year in which the Korean Church was founded) and was a key leader in the Pyongyang Great Revival (1907-1910).

J. Edwin Orr, quoting the revivalist Charles Finney and the historian Beardsley said that the Southern States and the Southern people were not affected during this revival, but he disagreed with their findings. Edwin Orr wrote: 'There is good reason to believe that the revivals were as widespread in the South as in the Northern States. Allowances should be made for the fact that the South possessed no great industrial cities like the Northern metropolitan areas, and that her population was scattered over an agricultural countryside; hence it was less spectacular down South, where the newspaper could not immediately influence the crowded cities as in the North.' Edwin Orr quotes Bishop Candler (who documented the revivals in the Confederate Armies during the Civil War (1861-1865) which was over the very issue of slavery) and stated that the 'results of the [1857-1859] revival "were in proportion to the population, greater in the South than in any other section."[17]

In 1876, William W. Bennett wrote *A Narrative of The Great Revival which Prevailed in the Southern Armies* of which 'the facts of the army revival are stated by those who witnessed them.'[17]

Gold Coast Revival (1875-1878)

In 1661, Cape Coast, on the Gold Coast of West Africa (modern day Ghana) passed from the Dutch into British hands which included the white turreted Cape Coast Castle. During 1835-1837, four European missionaries from the Wesleyan Missionary Society arrived in quick succession at Cape Coast but most died within a few months and no one lasted two years.

In 1809, Thomas Birch Freeman was born in Twyford, England. His dad was a freed slave; believed to be from the West Indies (via Africa) who lived in his former master's (John Birch's) household. Thomas Freeman's mother was a European serving woman in the same household. Thomas' father died when he was six. His mother remarried and Thomas was brought up with his mother in John Birch's household who educated him well. Thomas was converted as a youth under the Methodists. Sir Robert Harland and Lady Harland took great interest in Thomas, helping him improve his education, especially in the areas of botany and horticulture and he was made head gardener at Orwell Park under Sir Harland's ownership. But when Sir Harland found out that Thomas had joined himself to the Methodists as a preacher, he was given an ultimatum with a month to think it over – your job or your preaching?! He resigned much to Lady Harland's vexation.

In 1837, Thomas Freeman offered his service to the Wesleyan Missionary Society for the Gold Coast of West Africa (modern day Ghana, Togo, Benin and South West Nigeria) and was advised to marry. This was a recent missionary requirement for this area, as all the pioneering Wesleyan missionaries had quickly suffered illness and ultimate death within months, or no more than two years of service due to the climate. Thomas married Miss Boot, the lady housekeeper at Orwell Park.

In January 1838, they arrived at Cape Coast to find that the last missionary had died in November 1837. There was an established church of around fifty natives plus a boys and girls school. His wife died within two months of arrival. Thomas Freeman, remarried in November 1840, but in August 1841, she died and passed into glory.

Thomas Freeman, first saw revival on the Gold Coast (Ghana) from 1851-1852. In 1851, a court case put Christianity on trial against paganism, and the former won. New churches were built and sacred groves were cut down as revival swept along the Gold Coast. J. Milum who wrote about Thomas Freeman's life and spent time with him (in Freeman's old age) wrote: 'Close upon the trial…a gracious wave of revival swept over the mission. All the stations of the Gold Coast seemed to have been more or less visited. Mr Freeman was incessant in the glorious toil. At Anamabu [also spelt Anomabo, approximately ten miles from Cape Coast along the Gold Coast in modern day Ghana] he was called upon to receive a number of adults by baptism into the Church. These catechumens had all been prepared by long trial.' Thomas Freeman wrote: 'They thronged the communion rail four deep and I found at the conclusion that I had baptised eighty-two adults…It was indeed a delightful scene to witness.'

A love-feast was held at Cape Coast in 1852 which concluded 'a series of remarkable meetings.' At a sacramental service, 'the crowds were so great that it was approaching eleven o'clock at night before the service concluded' and the day had begun with a 5am prayer meeting![1]

Thomas Freeman's pioneering work lasted nearly fifty years of service amongst fierce tribes, fetish priests, native kings and their customs; the cruel inhuman rituals of human sacrifice and slavery for profit. Thomas laboured under the Wesleyan Missionary Society (WMS) from 1838 until he 'reluctantly severed his connections with the mission in 1858.' His work was 'so successful' that the mission stations he opened (along three hundred miles of coastline (and inland), from Dixcove in Ghana, to Lagos in Nigeria) 'involved an embarrassing outlay upon the missionary committee' and conditions were laid down which he could not comply with.

After leaving the WMS, he "retired" to Accra (capital of Ghana) with his third wife (a native) and they had at least two sons. For sixteen years, he rested; but grew fruit for the Europeans, sent rare orchids to Kew Gardens in England, but still frequently filled the pulpits of the WMS churches and took an active interest in the society. In 1873, he returned to the WMS and was given charge of a mission at Anamabu 'and under his fostering care the cause marvellously prospered.'[2]

In 1874, the Ashanti War broke out and the British government were obliged to send troops under Sir Garnett Wolseley (alongside native contingents) to suppress the rebellion. Thomas Freeman was commandeered by the General (with the WMS permission) to furnish information, which compromised his position. Coomassie, the capital of Ashanti (inhabited by

40,000 natives, just a few decades previously) was left in ruins – thus ended the war and Freeman was released. Smallpox had ravaged the Gold Coast a few years previously and alongside the war had prepared the inhabitants, by 'chastening the people' and 'doubtless prepared them for a gracious work' of the Holy Spirit which spread along the Gold Coast.

In early October 1875, Thomas Freeman visited Kuntu, an outstation of Anamabu, where he found the Christians greatly quickened and in great spiritual expectancy. He wrote: 'During the preaching the people were moved and cried aloud. As they knelt penitently at the communion rail, many trembled exceedingly, and clutched the rail to prevent their falling, such was their deep emotion.' A few days later communion was conducted at Anamabu where three hundred partook. In the same month, Thomas Freeman visited Cape Coast, and alongside the native minister, Andrew W. Parker, a special meeting was conducted for penitents. Thomas Freeman wrote: 'Such was the gracious influence resting on the people that cries of mercy resounded through the schoolroom.' Many found the peace of God and the other seekers moved to a house and continued all night in prayer! At Salt Pond and Accra (seventy miles apart) similar scenes were witnessed as the churches were too full and people spilled out onto the streets.

At Elmina, (twenty miles from Cape Coast), in company with the Rev. George Dyer (recently arrived from England) and the native ministers, Messieurs Laing and Parker, 'a notable service was held – such a meeting had never been known in Elmina.' The chapel was full to capacity as people stood outside, pressed round the open door and windows. Thomas Freeman wrote: 'There was a gracious influence resting on the congregation. We invited the penitents to the communion rail, to which they came in crowds. The Blessed Spirit brooded over us, and we had a fine revival meeting. Scores of the congregation were in tears and crying for mercy and many found peace and joy in believing.

At Great Kormantine (on the Gold Coast), the people 'cried mightily to the Lord for salvation.' Leaving the chapel, Thomas Freeman preached to the fishermen in the open air, 'who were greatly moved by the truths declared' and then retired to the chapel to perform three weddings. One wedding was delayed by a few hours, as in the morning prayer meeting, 'one of the young brides-elect had fallen insensible on the floor under the hallowed fervour…'

In 1838, the Wesleyan Cape Coast Church (190 miles from Accra), was built on an elevated position and consisted of four thousand large white stones. It could hold between 700 to 1,000 people on the ground floor, with two commodious vestries, though the opening service in June 1838, saw 1,200 natives cram inside and galleries were added at a later date, 'and was the scene of many spiritual revivals' during both Gold Coast Revivals. In 1875, such were the numbers now attending the Wesleyan Cape Coast Church that discussions commenced about enlarging it but it was wisely decided that the boys' school should be used as an overflow chapel.[3]

At this time, Thomas Freeman's wife wrote to him from Anamabu, asking him to return as the chapel congregation was overflowing into the streets – she wrote: 'Please try and come down again...Many had to sit outside; it is wonderful. I have never seen anything like this at any time.' A few days later she wrote: 'While one girl was praying and crying all that were in the chapel trembled...' In still another letter she wrote: 'One of our sisters, reports that, as she was passing along the street, she met a group of about twelve heathen people, men and women, from the fishermen's quarter of the town, who were saying, "We will go to chapel to be Christians; we will go and give ourselves to God omnipotent." ' Then followed a series of remarkable services at Anamabu, where as at Cape Coast, the schoolroom was used for overflow crowds; as 'a chapel-of-ease to accommodate the crowds that came.'

In early December 1875, Freeman revisited Salt Pond (twenty miles from Cape Coast), where the candidates for baptism, occupied a line of benches forty-seven paces long. On the same day he returned to Anamabu where two hundred and twelve people were baptised in the presence of hundreds – three hundred in total were baptised in one day!

New Year Eve's watch-night service at Anamabu was special. Thomas Freeman wrote: 'A crowded congregation... At midnight a mighty influence rested on the congregation. Stifled sobs soon rose into loud cries all over the chapel. Oh, what a scene! At length I succeeded in giving out and raising the hymn, 'Sing to the Great Jehovah's Praise.' We sang it through, but in the midst of cries and tears strangely mingled with the harmony.' The meeting ended at 12.30am, but the people would not leave, so the leaders started a prayer meeting which lasted until 3.30am. The following day, 1 January 1876, in accordance with Methodist custom, a solemn covenant service was held and about five hundred partook of communion.

J. Milum stated that 'there were many extraordinary cases' of people trembling violently, loud cries, 'which might rank with some recorded in John Wesley's *Journals*.' He describes one case – 'and there were many of a similar character which occurred at Anamabu by public baptism' and then quotes Freeman who said, "One female adult was much excited at the communion rail, first trembling violently, and at length breaking out into loud cries as though under intense bodily or mental suffering. She seemed to lose her power of volition, and had to be taken out of the chapel by some of her friends who were present." Later on, Thomas Freeman warned his church leader about excesses and advised them how to act during the revival. 'Less the people come to think that loud cries and trembling as a necessary part, or as adjuncts to conversion.'

On the 20 January 1876, Thomas Freeman married five couples and 'baptised two hundred and sixty adults' and children...Whole households were baptised.' One of the later candidates for baptism was the head of a pagan family who was formerly an extravagant drinker of rum, ale, wine and other intoxicants which was connected as part of a ritual with the burial of the dead. Freeman wrote: 'These are the blessed changes now effected by the operations of the Holy Spirit. Glory to God!'

On the 9 April 1876, Great Kormantine (on the Gold Coast) became host to the first Camp Meeting in West Africa (possibly Africa!). Before dawn, people started arriving for the 10am worship, where one thousand people were present. After the service, the people dispersed into groups and had breakfast. Thomas Freeman wrote: '...That being over, several large groups collected for exhortations, prayer and praise. This was a beautiful scene, the culminating point of the day. Over an extent ground of three or four hundred yards square, dotted with clumps of cocoanut palms in every direction the voice of prayer and praise was heard, while others were walking in the open spaces engaged in earnest conversation.' Fifteen hundred people partook of the love-feast in the afternoon.

In September 1876, another Camp Meeting was held at Great Kormantine where the people gathered in greater numbers than before – Thomas Freeman estimated that there were about two thousand present. The Camp Meeting was held also in 1878. Thomas Freeman, in reference to the Camp Meetings said, "It may be deemed important to notice that the extraordinary meetings in feeding the revival has been their suitableness to the national genius of the people. In their pagan life they are accustomed to frequent and extensive gatherings in their occasional and annual customs. Thus the national habits have been utilised to promote the spread of the Gospel, and to uplift the Church of Christ into a higher atmosphere of Christian life."

At the end of 1877, at least three thousand people had been added to the Church and fifteen hundred had been baptised by Thomas Freeman himself. J Milum wrote: 'These, added to the baptism of the previous year, showed an increase of some four thousand five hundred, and still the gracious revival continued.'[4]

In his old age, Thomas Freeman, though disguised under another name, wrote about the lonely missionary trials and victories which was a picture of his own life. It revealed his early beginning and the fruits that followed: 'Newly arrived in the burning climate of torrid Africa...Will he stand firm in the day of battle?...Surrounded by perishing people who have not seen the life-inspiring vision, he has no human aid at hand, no earthly friend or counsellor. Now comes the test of faith and patience. Like the husbandman, he must wait for the precious fruits and have long patience until the Lord sends the early and refreshing rain. Yes, he must toil on through many a dark, cloudy day, ploughing and sowing in hope. Bearer of the precious seed, he will doubtless weep, for he is indeed in the vale of tears; but faith beholds in the distance the time of rejoicing amidst the glorious harvest...Onward then, our beloved missionary! Onward, lonely messenger of mercy, warrior of Messiah, greatly valorous! When thy hands hang down and thy spirit droops, remember Calvary...'[5]

In 1883, Thomas Freeman 'met with unprecedented success at Accra. He had formed evangelistic bands, which were doing a good work, and reported the conversion of an Ashanti prince from Juabin, named Akympon, who had become an unpaid evangelist.'

In 1886, Father Freeman (as he was known in old age) was advised to retire from active work and became the supernumerary minister in Accra and resorted to tending his garden. In May 1890, he caught a cold; on the 6 August he caught influenza and on the 11 August 1890, in the presence of his eldest son, he passed into glory.[6]

Azusa Street Revival (1906-1909)

The Azusa Street Revival, also known as the Azusa Street Outpouring, broke out in Los Angeles, California, America, a little over one century ago. This revival brought about a fresh touch of the Holy Spirit, bringing disciples the new awareness of the old truth of the baptism in the Holy Spirit.

Evangelist (and journalist) Frank Bartleman documented this move of God and some of the streams that led up to the dam of revival breaking forth. This flowed across Los Angeles and went worldwide, ushering in the worldwide twentieth century Pentecostal renewal. At the centenary of the Azusa Street Revival, it was estimated that there were over 600 million Pentecostals worldwide!

Before the Azusa Street Revival, there was an air of expectancy amongst Christians. This led to a general excitement and hunger for the things of God and prayer meetings were commenced for seeking the blessing in various quarters. Revivals broke out in Houston, Texas, Kansas City and Pasadena, Los Angeles, where believers were being baptised in the Holy Spirit.

Frank Bartleman arrived in Los Angeles, nearing the end of December 1904 with his wife and two young daughters. Within two weeks, their eldest child Esher, aged three, died. At the graveside, Frank Bartleman, with a broken heart, pledged his life afresh to God. Within one week he began working in Christian ministry, preaching twice a day at the Peniel Mission Hall in Pasadena, Los Angeles. He also began to evangelise and to distribute tracts wherever he could, including banks, post offices, drinking saloons and houses of prostitution.

In the second week of April 1905, Frank Bartleman heard F. B. Meyer of London, England, preaching about the Welsh Revival (1904-1905). Meyer had just come from Wales and had met Evan Roberts. After hearing the stirring reports, Bartleman fully surrendered his life to the Lord and resolved that God would be able to use him as he longed to see revival.

At the beginning of May 1905, 'a powerful revival broke out' in the Lake Avenue M. E. Church, Pasadena. Most of the young male converts from the Peniel Mission were active in the church and had been praying for revival. Every night people were converted to the Lord Jesus Christ and on one night, 'nearly every unsaved soul in the house was converted…Conviction was mightily upon the people.' Within two weeks, there were 200 new Christians and the church began to pray for revival not only for Pasadena, but for Los Angeles and the whole of Southern California.

In May 1905, Frank Bartleman was given the book *The Great Revival In Wales* by S. B. Shaw. After reading it, he resolved to give up his secular employment as a journalist and became a channel in which the burden for revival could come upon. He also distributed 5,000 pamphlets, *The Revival in Wales* by G. Campbell Morgan. Frank Bartleman wrote numerous articles on revival (exhorting the brethren to pray) which were published in various church and religious papers. He began selling S. B. Shaw's book, amongst the churches that he spoke at and 'God wonderfully used it to promote faith for a revival spirit.' Soon the spirit of revival consumed Frank Bartleman and he was joined in prayer with Edward Boehmer, a convert of the Peniel Mission.

In May 1905, Frank Bartleman wrote to Evan Roberts (of the Welsh Revival 1904-1905), asking him (and the Welsh people) to pray for the brethren in California and he received a reply stating that they were. In June, Frank Bartleman wrote again to Evan Robert's asking for continued prayer. Prior to the outbreak at Azusa, Frank Bartleman wrote to Evan Roberts three times and received four responses.

Frank Bartleman visited Joseph Smale's church, the First Baptist Church, Los Angeles, in mid June. Smale, was on fire for the Lord and his church was praying for revival. He had just returned from Wales, where the revival fires were raging and had met Evan Roberts. Within a few weeks, Smale's church was filled with people who were 'anticipating wonderful things.' Soul travail and a fear of God began to come upon the people and some of the services would continue until the early hours. Frank Bartleman wrote: 'A wonderful work of the Spirit has broken out here...preceded by a deep and preparatory work of prayer and anticipation. Conviction is rapidly spreading among the people.' The revival lasted for fifteen weeks, until the leaders of the church wanted to return to the old order. Smale resigned and many followed him as he founded a new church in the area.[1]

William Seymour, a one-eyed African American from Texas, became the best-known human personality of the revival, but the Holy Spirit was in charge. Some of the other people connected with the Azusa Street Revival (and / or the life of

Seymour) were: Charles Parham, Frank Bartleman, William Durham, Joseph Smale, Florence Crawford and Lucy Farrow.

William Seymour was invited to be a pastor of a Holiness Church on Santa Fe Street in Los Angeles, but as soon as he started to preach on the baptism of the Holy Spirit, he was locked out of his church and his lodgings upstairs! He was taken in by some church members who agreed with his teaching (on the baptism of the Holy Spirit and holiness) and felt obligated to help him out. In his prayer closet he pressed in after the things of God. A prayer meeting was held at his new lodgings and he became known as a man of prayer.

In late February 1906, William Seymour moved to new lodgings in North Bonnie Brae Street and was invited to hold meetings there, and with a small group they began to pray and fast. One man was healed instantly after being anointed with oil by William Seymour; after a second prayer, the man began to speak in tongues, and people soon flocked to this house church. As the spiritual fire from heaven descended, many witnesses believed the house itself was literally on fire and the fire brigade was called out! It was not until April 1906 that Seymour began to speak in tongues.[2]

In late March 1906, Frank Bartleman first met William Seymour at a cottage meeting and then began to attend the meetings at Bonnie Brae Street.

On the 18 April 1906, the San Francisco earthquake shook the ground for under one minute; five hundred people were killed in San Francisco. The surrounding cities and country were devastated. The next day, a small earthquake hit Los Angeles, 'it was an earnest time' and people were afraid. Frank Bartleman felt led to attend the Azusa Street Mission which had just moved from Bonnie Brae Street and he gave his first sermon there. The earthquake had opened many hearts to eternal issues. The vast majority of preachers were trying to calm the fears of the people, stating that the earthquake was from the devil and not of God. Frank Bartleman view was the complete opposite; he told the people that it was God's judgment and a wakeup call – 'the voice of God to the people on the Pacific Coast.' Frank Bartleman had a faith ministry in writing and distributing tracts and on the 22 April 1906, 10,000 tracts, *The Last Call* were rapidly distributed around the city from workers of The New Testament Church (Burbank Hall) which had begun under Joseph Smale. In May, the Lord gave him a tract called the *Earthquake* and with the aid of helpers,

75,000 were given out in three weeks, and another 50,000 at Oakland, Bay Cities, under F. W. Manley in the same period of time.[3]

In April 1906, William Seymour's house church had found new premises on 312 Azusa Street because the crowds grew too big! The building (formerly a Methodist church) was made of wood. It had been previously used as a stable and store house for several years and was therefore in quite a state of disrepair. People flocked to the building where sawdust covered the floor. When people arrived, greetings were kept to a minimum, the people wanted to meet with God. There were two floors, the upper was known as the "Tarrying Room" where people waited on God to be baptised in the Holy Spirit (based on Luke 24:49 from the Authorised Version), though many also received this blessing downstairs in the main hall.

In the beginning of the Azusa Mission, they had no musical instruments or hymn books, as they felt no need for them, all was spontaneous – there was no prearranged programme to rush through. Someone would give a testimony, sing or read some passages of Scripture and eventually someone would preach, regardless of age, colour or gender. All the well known hymns were sung from memory quickened by the Spirit of God and especially the song, 'The Comforter Has Come.' There was much emphasis on the blood of Jesus. All sorts of people flocked to Azusa, including crooks, cranks, religious soreheads, presumptuous men, spiritualists, and hypnotists, many with evil spirits who came to influence the work. The press gave very bad reports, but this only gave free advertisement to the movement. There were foes inside and outside of the Azusa Mission Hall and as Frank Bartleman wrote: 'Discernment was not perfect.' This led to the work being reproached, 'but the saints soon learnt to take the precious from the vile…The fight was terrific.' People received their deliverance from demons and were liberated in the mighty name of Jesus. Many were also slain by the Spirit of God and 'were carried out dead, spiritually speaking' (in a comatose state) from the meetings.

By August 1906, the police had been asked to break up the meetings! William Seymour sometimes preached behind a wooden box, but as the move of God progressed, he was frequently found praying on his knees behind the box as the Holy Spirit did what He wanted to. The meetings became spontaneous, as the place was steeped in prayer and intercession and the Shekinah glory (Divine mist) was present at every meeting! Services lasted for hours, half a day, or continued all night and the doors were not locked, impromptu services ran day and night, led by the Holy Spirit. Anybody who had a message stood up and spoke and this was open to abuse. Intellectuals and those of the flesh began to preach, but as the brethren prayed, they would quickly lose their train of thought, or fluster over words and would be humbled in the dust by the Holy Spirit. At the beginning no altar calls were given, 'God Himself would call them.'

At one evening meeting, a Baptist preacher, Ansel Post was sat on a chair in the middle of the floor. The Holy Spirit fell on him; he sprang to his feet and began to praise God in tongues. Being filled with Divine love he 'ran all over the place, hugging all the brethren he could get hold of.' He later went to Egypt as a missionary.[4]

In the early days of Azusa, Frank Bartleman received more than five hundred letters from people enquiring about the revival, most of whom were well known teachers and preachers. Fearing pride, he burnt them all in 1911, and later regretted doing so as they would have been of great 'historical evidence to the widespread influence of the revival.'[5]

One author wrote: 'In the early Azusa days both heaven and hell seemed to have come to town...There was much persecution, especially from the press. The place was packed out nightly. The colour line was washed away in the blood.'[6]

Eventually the meetings were held three times a day – morning, afternoon, and night. Tongues-speaking was the central blessing which attracted multitudes of curious people, but healing of the sick soon followed (even creative miracles) and the walls were soon covered with the crutches and canes of those who had been miraculously healed. The gift of tongues was soon followed by the gift of interpretation.[7]

Train loads of passengers from across the States came to experience this new move of God. People enroute to the meeting would be prostrated; some would rise and speak in tongues, others were under conviction of sin and this was two to three blocks away! Even Frank Bartleman stated that more than once, within two blocks of Azusa Mission, he had to stop and pray for strength to go on as the presence of God was so real. Many people saw Divine fire coming out off the roof of the Azusa Mission, and descending from the heavens and meeting in the sky! By the summer of 1906, thousands of people were turning up and were being blessed by God.

On Friday June 15 1906, 'At Azusa the Spirit dropped the "heavenly chorus" into my soul...no one could understand this "gift of song" but those who had it. It was indeed a "new song" in the Spirit...the Lord has sovereignly bestowed it, with the outpouring of the "residue of oil" the latter rain baptism of the Spirit. It was exercised as the Spirit moved the possessors, either in solo fashion, or by the company. It was sometimes without words, other times in "tongues"...it brought about a heavenly atmosphere, as though the angels themselves were present and joining with us...this "new song" was altogether different, not of human composition. It cannot be successfully counterfeited. The crow cannot imitate the dove. But they finally began to despise this "gift" when the human spirit asserted itself again. They drove it out by hymn books, and selected songs by leaders. It was like murdering the Spirit, and most painful to some of us, but the tide was too strong against us.'[8]

In September 1906, a local newspaper reporter frowned on the events taking place and wrote that the Azusa Street mission was a 'disgraceful intermingling of the races...they cry and make howling noises all day and into the night. They run, jump, shake all over, shout to the top of their voice, spin around in circles, fall out on the sawdust blanketed floor jerking, kicking and rolling all over it. Some of them pass out and do not move for hours as though they were dead. These people appear to be mad, mentally deranged or under a spell. They claim to be filled with the Spirit. They have a one eyed, illiterate, Negro as their preacher who stays on his knees much of the time with his head hidden between the wooden milk crates. He doesn't talk very much but at times he can be heard shouting, 'Repent,' and he's supposed to be running the thing...They repeatedly sing the same song, 'The Comforter Has Come.' '[9]

Frank Bartleman wrote: 'The truth must be told. Azusa began to fail the Lord early in her ministry.' In the second week of August 1906, a sign had been painted on the outside of the Azusa Mission, 'Apostolic Faith Mission' which labelled it as part of a denomination and would in time give way to a sectarian spirit with its rules and ecclesiastical regulation, thus quenching the Spirit. Frank Bartleman wrote: 'From that time the trouble and division began. It was no longer a free Spirit for all as it had been.'[10] By this time there were three other Missions in the immediate vicinity, two of whom were open to the Holy Spirit and were encouraging all those present to seek their own Pentecost. The three Missions were the New Testament Church under Pastor Smale (which was not open to the Spirit anymore), the Upper Room Mission at 327 South Spring Street under Elmer Fisher (a Spirit filled group who split from Smale and most of the white saints from Azusa Mission, also followed him) and the church at Eighth and Maple Street under Pastors Frank Barleman and Pastor Pendelton, though in less than two months, Frank Bartleman, due to fatigue, handed the church over to Pendelton. Pastor Pendelton at the end of August 1906, along with forty of members of his congregation had been expelled from their denomination because they spoke in tongues and the leadership had intended to try him for heresy! So, Frank Bartleman invited him to the church building he was renting where services were held every evening. Azusa was always seen as the mother Mission and Frank Bartleman and William Seymour used to visit back and forth, there was never any jealousy or friction between them.[11]

In September 1906, *The Apostolic Faith* (Azusa Paper) published its first report of the revival. One of the articles titled Old-Time Pentecost talk about the history of modern Pentecost: 'This work began about five years ago last January [1901], when a company of people under the leadership of Charles Parham, who were studying God's word, tarried for Pentecost, in Topeka [Bible School] Kansas. After searching through the country everywhere, they had been unable to find any Christians that had the true Pentecostal power. So they laid aside all commentaries and notes and waited on the Lord, studying His Word, and what they did not understand they got down before the bench and asked God to have wrought out in their hearts by the Holy Ghost. They had a prayer tower from which prayers were ascending night and day to God. After three months, a sister [Miss Agnes Ozman] who had been teaching sanctification for the baptism of the Holy Spirit, one who had a sweet, loving experience and all the carnality taken out of her heart, felt the Lord lead her to have hands laid on her to receive the Pentecost. So when they prayed [in the evening of the 31 December 1900], the Holy Ghost came in great power and she commenced speaking in an unknown tongue. This made all the Bible School hungry, and three nights afterward, twelve students received the Holy Ghost, and prophesied, and cloven tongues could be seen upon their heads. They then had an experience that measured up with the second chapter of Acts, and could understand the first chapter of Ephesians.

'Now after five years something like 13,000 people have received this Gospel. It is spreading everywhere, until churches who do not believe backslide and lose the experience they have.'[12]

Eventually things turned bad at Azusa, people accused William Seymour of starting a new denomination. There were many misunderstandings and new ideas being thrown about which generally led to confusion and frustration, while others were working it up in the flesh. One of the misconceptions of tongues was that some who felt called to the mission field believed that they already had the ability to speak in another nation's language and were devastated on arrival at their mission field. Though at the meetings when some people spoke in tongues, others nationalities heard them speaking in their mother tongue and were converted because of this sign from heaven!

By 1909, Frank Bartleman's account of the Apostolic Faith Mission (Azusa Mission) was not good. He had spent the previous year ministering across America and in 1909 visited the Hawaiian Islands. At Azusa, everything was run in a set order and those present came into more and more bondage, it was a 'spirit of dictatorship.' The following year, Bartleman embarked on an eleven month world tour, living by faith (as he had done since, he fully surrendered himself to the Lord) and returned in late February 1911. One week before he arrived, William H. Durham, a former Baptist minister, from the North Avenue Mission in Chicago, began to hold meetings at Azusa and revival broke out once again! It was known by many as the 'second shower of the Latter Rain' and on one Sunday, five hundred people were turned away! But, on the 2 May 1911, the doors to the Apostolic Faith Mission were locked with a chain and padlock. William Seymour had been preaching in the east of America and the trustees of the Mission quickly summoned him back. They had decided to lock Durham out because they objected to his message. Durham then rented a large building at Seventh and Los Angeles Street and on a Sunday, 1,000 people would attend, with four hundred on a weeknight. He received much opposition and in the winter returned to Chicago where he was wonderfully used of God. He caught a cold and died of influenza after returning to Los Angeles in 1912.[13]

Pyongyang Great Revival (1907-1910)

The first Protestant missionary to Korea was a Welshman, the Rev. Robert Jermain Thomas. He first arrived in the Hermit Kingdom in 1865 and secretly spent four months there. In 1866 he returned and sold classical Chinese Bibles (which could be read by Koreans, Japanese and Chinese) and risked decapitation if caught. Korea was still a closed land to foreigners though in 1876 she started diplomatic relations with Japan who first introduced foreign products into Korea.

On the 2 September 1866, Rev. Robert Jermain Thomas was martyred on the river bank (alongside all the crew of the merchant-marine schooner that he was travelling on) outside of Pyongyang (see Appendix B) and is the present capital of North Korea and the centre where the 1907 revival broke out.[1]

In 1877, J. Ross and J. McIntyre published a Korean grammar book called *Corean Primer*. Some missionaries (who were not based in Korea) first translated and published the *Gospel of Luke* in Korean in 1882 with the help of Korean assistants, Lee Woong-Chan, Baek Hong-Jun, Kim Jin-Gi, Choi Seong-Gyun and Seo Sang-Ryun.

In September 1884, N. Allen, an American medical missionary arrived in Seoul under the Treaty of Amity and Commerce between America and Korea, which though it did not mention the freedom of church (there was no church), did enable people (tentmaker missionaries) to be involved in social work, establishing schools, relief houses and medical work etc.

On Easter Day 1885, two American missionaries, H. G. Underwood, a Presbyterian and Henry G. Appenzeller, a Methodist, landed in Incheon Port, Korea. With the help of Korean language instructors they translated the *Gospel of Mark* which was published in Yokohama, Japan in 1887.

The year 1885 is officially recognised as the founding of the Korean Church and in 2005, they celebrated their one hundred and twentieth anniversary. The Korean New Testament was published in 1887, (though it had already been published in Manchuria by others in 1882). The translation of the Old Testament begun in 1906 under the Bible Translation Committee which in 1887, had been jointly organised by H. G. Underwood and H. G. Appenzeller who had published their New Testament translation in 1900 based on the Chinese,

English and Greek versions. The Old Testament was complete in 1910 and published in 1911.

H. G. Appenzeller laid the foundation for modern education by establishing Paicha School and Chungdong First Church. In 1902 he drowned, along with his assistant Jo Han-Gyu after the ship he was travelling in collided with another ship due to fog.[2]

In 1886, the first Protestant Korean was baptised and by 1887 there were seven Korean converts.[3] Korea saw its first revival in 1903 and it was known as the Wonsan Revival Movement and both the Presbyterians and Methodists reaped large harvests as they were united to exalt Jesus Christ. In 1904, there were 10,000 converts in Pyongyang and by the middle of 1906, after 30,000 new converts in that year alone, the revival had waned and died out.

Professor Samuel H. Moffet of Princeton Theological Seminary was the son of Samuel A. Moffet, missionary to Jangdaehyun Presbyterian Church, Pyongyang (where revival broke out in 1907). Professor Samuel, in an interview in the early twenty-first century stated that in 1906 there were at least 30,000 new converts in the Pyongyang area alone, "maybe a little larger" but also said, "30,000 baptisms don't always mean 30,000 new Christians" and it was the revival the following year which really showed them what the Gospel meant.[4]

Pyongyang in 1907 was known as a city of wine, women and song. It was a dark city in the early twentieth century with sin abounding. It even had its own Gisaeng (Korean geisha) training school. It was in this city that Korea's second revival began in January 1907 after months of persistent prayer, 50,000 people were converted in that one year and Korea was set ablaze – it was known as the Pyongyang Great Revival. Missionary, John McCune in a letter wrote: '...The work of the Holy Spirit here [at the Jangdaehyun Church] would far surpass what we have read about the great revival in Wales and India.'[5]

At the beginning of the Japanese Russian War of 1904, American missionaries were initially confined to Pyongyang by government order and Korea (but especially Pyongyang) was overrun by Japanese troops passing through. The missionaries needed a special Japanese / English passport to travel to their outlying country churches. In the autumn of 1906 when the threat of Russian invasion had passed the Japanese did not withdraw which caused anxiety amongst the population who historically had constantly been fought over by Japan or China, its people were suppressed and then oppressed. William

Newton Blair, a missionary at Pyongyang wrote: 'With the Japanese occupation accomplished, patriotism was born in Korea.'

At the same time a number of young Korean 'big heads' returned from America and caused problems amongst the American missionaries with their personal ambition and true stories of American corruption which they saw with their own eyes. Some stated that the American missionaries were no different and that Korea's problems were all American instigated. Also, America, following Britain's example 'hastened to recognise Japan's control' which caused an anti-American sentiment to sweep over the land.

In 1907, the Korean Church (Presbyterian) was to become independent of its American Board of Foreign Mission which had been 'practically self-supporting for several years.' The missionaries were now very concerned that if they did hand over authority to the fledgling Presbyterian Church, it could fall apart. In August 1906, the Pyongyang missionaries met for a week of Bible study and prayer. They invited Dr. R. A. Hardie, (also spelt Hardy) to lead them, whose public confession and repentance in Wonsan in 1903 was the beginning of the Wonsan Revival Movement (1903-1906).

Their text book for the meeting was the First Epistle of John. The apostle John wrote that everything depended upon fellowship with God, and that Divine fellowship was conditional upon love and righteousness. William Newton Blair wrote that the message became personal and living: 'We had reached a place where we dared not go forward without God's presence.' The missionaries poured out their hearts before Him, and searched their own hearts while seeking to meet the conditions. Before the meeting had ended the Spirit showed those present that 'the way of victory' is the way of, 'confession, of broken hearts and bitter tears.'

They decided to pray for 'a great blessing' a revival amongst their Korean brethren and especially amongst the annual Pyongyang Bible-study classes for men which would take place in January 1907. They left those August meetings 'realising as never before that nothing but the baptism of the God's Spirit in mighty power could fit us and our Korean brethren for the trying days ahead.' They knew that the Korean Church needed to repent of hating the Japanese and needed 'a clearer vision of all sin against God' because many had professed Christ as their Saviour 'without great sorrow for sin because of its familiarity.'[6]

In September 1906, Dr. Howard Agnew Johnston, of New York, whilst in Seoul, informed a group of missionaries and Korean Christians about the Khasi Hills Revival (1905-1906) in India. See *The Revival in the Khasia Hills* by Mrs John Roberts (1906). Jonathan Goforth, a missionary based in China (who also ministered in Manchuria) wrote that because of this more than twenty missionaries from Ping Yang (Pyongyang) Presbyterian and Methodist missions resolved to meet together to pray daily for 'greater blessings.' Over the Christmas period the Pyongyang Christians met each evening for prayer, instead of their usual festive celebrations. The evening prayer ceased at the start of the Pyongyang General Class but continued at noon for those who could attend.

A Bible colporteur from Kan Kai Church along the Yalu River, of 250 believers was also in Seoul. He heard Dr. Johnston and encouraged his church to meet for prayer at 5am through the autumn and winter of 1906-1907. For six months they prayed until the Holy Spirit 'came as a flood.'[7]

The Bible-study class system was a Korean feature where each church appointed a week or longer where all normal work was laid aside. William Newton Blair wrote: 'The result of such uninterrupted Bible study in inevitably a quickening of the entire Church, a true revival of love and service.' Beside the classes held in each church, representatives from all the churches in one district met at the General Class which last from ten days to two weeks where Bible studies and conferences were held.

The Pyongyang General Class of one thousand began on the 2 January 1907, it would last for two weeks and representatives came from as far away as one hundred miles. This was one of the reasons why the revival spread so far and fast, as revived Christians, 'fire carriers' travelled back to their churches and caught them alight – revival by extension.

The evening meetings began on Saturday the sixth and 1,500 attended. William Newton Blair preached on 1 Corinthians 12:27 (members of the body of Christ), and exhorted those present to get right with one another, 'as discord in the Church was like sickness in the body.' After the sermon 'a number with sorrow confessed their lack of love for others, especially for the Japanese...many testified to a new realisation of what sin was.'

The Sunday evening meeting had no life in it and the missionaries were 'conscious that the devil had been present, apparently victorious.' The next day the missionaries met 'and cried out to God in earnest, they were 'bound in spirit and refused to let go till He blessed' them. As the people (and only some of the missionaries) entered the church at 7pm God's presence was felt. After a short sermon, missionary Graham Lee led the meeting in prayer and soon, 'the whole audience began to pray out loud together.' It was 'a vast harmony of sound and spirit, a mingling together of souls moved by an irresistible impulse to prayer.'[8]

Jonathan Goforth, missionary to China and Manchuria visited eight chief mission centres in Korea for three weeks during June 1907. In his brief account of the revival he stated that Elder *Keel of the Central Presbyterian Church was the catalyst of the revival when he confessed his sin of 'Achan' (see Joshua 7:1, 20-21) in front of 1,500 people. *Also spelt Kil and he was later known as the Rev. Sun Joo Kil. He had promised a dying man to look after his estate because his wife was unable to, but in the process he had taken one hundred dollars for himself. After confessing this sin he returned the money to the widow the following day.[9]

Soon the prayer turned to weeping. Graham Lee wrote: 'Man after man would rise, confess his sins, break down and weep, and then throw himself to the floor and beat the floor with his fists in perfect agony of conviction.' The meeting went on till 2am. Jonathan Goforth wrote: 'Day after day the people assembled now, and always it was manifest that the Refiner was in His temple.'

On Tuesday afternoon the whole community assembled to give thanks to God. The previous night, Elder Kang You-moon, of the Central Church confessed his hatred of Elder Kim, who was William Newton Blair's assistant in the Pyongyang Church. Elder Kim sat silent. At the noon prayer meeting on Tuesday they prayed for Elder Kim. In the evening meeting, Elder Kim stood behind the pulpit and confessed his hatred not only of Elder Kang, but also of William Blair himself and asked for Blair's forgiveness. William Blair began to pray, "Father, Father" and got no further. William Blair wrote: 'It seemed as if the roof was lifted from the building and the Spirit of God came down from heaven in a mighty avalanche of power upon us.' William Blair fell at Elder Kim's side and wept and prayed as never before. Some prostrated themselves before the Lord while hundreds stood with arms outstretched towards heaven. 'The cry went over the city until the heathen were in consternation.' The missionaries had prayed for an outpouring of the Spirit and it had come – Korea would never be the same again.

William Newton Blair wrote: 'Every sin a human being can commit was publicly confessed that night. Pale and trembling with emotion, in agony of mind and body, guilty souls, standing in the white light of that judgment, saw themselves as God saw them. Their sins rose up in all their vileness, till shame and grief and self-loathing took complete possession; pride was driven out, the face of men forgotten. Looking up to heaven, to Jesus whom they had betrayed, they smote themselves and cried out with bitter wailing, "Lord, Lord, cast us not away for ever!" '[10]

Jonathan Goforth in reference to Elder Keel's confession wrote: 'It hindered the Almighty God while it remained covered, and it glorified Him as soon as it was uncovered; and so with rare exceptions did all the confessions in Korea that year.'

In 1907, an old man, Chu Won Park, who attended a Presbyterian Church in Pyongyang, went to the front of the church and confessed that he had been the one who had killed Rev. Robert Jermain Thomas, forty-one years ago! Christians even confessed their sins to non-Christians for their past actions and attitudes which greatly affected the city. Even Japanese soldiers came under conviction! Soon Pyongyang became known as the "Jerusalem of the East."

Jonathan Goforth stated that in February 1907, revival broke out at the beginning of the Pyongyang High School of 318 students. The two missionaries in charge were praying in the principal's room because they 'wanted the Holy Spirit to control the school from the start.' Before 9am on that first Monday morning the Holy Spirit came and classes were suspended from Monday to Friday!

'Just then' Jonathan Goforth wrote 'about one hundred preachers and colporteurs of the Methodist Mission arrived in the city to study a month.' They got touched by the fire of God. A few days after the Methodist's left, '550 selected women from the Presbyterian country churches assembled in the city to study the Bible for twelve days. The Holy Spirit came and dealt with the women and transformed their lives.

'Scarcely had the women reached their homes [mid March 1907] when seventy-five new Presbyterian students in theology arrived to study three months' which was part of the five year course at the Pyongyang Theological Seminary. 'The Spirit did wonders.'[11]

In 1907, the Pyongyang Theological School graduated seven native Koreans who became the first Korean Presbytery of Korea. Bible study groups increased and there was an acceleration in missionary building growth. Illiterate people, especially women learnt the Hangeul script (Korean alphabet), and the understanding that God created all men equal in His eyes led to a greater status for women. The revival also crossed the border into Yeonbyeon and Manju, China.[12]

In Korea, every fifth day was a market day and the merchants would make more money on that day than on eight other days, but when the market fell on the Sabbath, 10,000 men and boys were found in the Sabbath School at Chung-Ju preferring to honour the Sabbath rather than make money.[13]

Mr Swallen who was one of more than twenty missionaries in Pyongyang said, "It paid well to have spent the several months in prayer, for when God the Holy Spirit came He accomplished more in half a day than all of us missionaries could have accomplished in half a year. In less than two months more than two thousand heathen were converted." Jonathan Goforth wrote: 'It is always so as soon as God gets first place; but as a rule, the Church, which professes to be Christ's, will not cease her busy round of activities and give God a chance by *waiting upon Him in prayer.*'[14]

Mr Swallen, Graham Lee (who was a good singer) and William Newton Blair were the main leaders prior to the revival, but it was Samuel Moffet and Kil Sun Mojo (this Korean rose before dawn to pray for revival) who brought them together from the missionary prayer meeting onward. During the revival, Elder Keel, who had confessed his sin of 'Achan' was raised up as a Korean leader. He held meetings everywhere and got the Koreans praying – a trait which the Koreans have never lost. He eventually became the pastor of Central Presbyterian Church, the church where he had confessed his sin which was the catalysis by his brokenness and repentance (backed by months of prayer by numerous people) for the Holy Spirit to descend.

Jonathan Goforth on his tour of the country in June 1907 said, "Those missionaries seemed to carry us right up to the throne of God. The Korean movement was of incalculable significance in my life, because it showed me at first hand the boundless possibilities of the revival method [to firstly see Christians revived and then the heathen saved]. Korea made me feel, as it did many others, that this was God's plan for setting the world aflame."[15] Jonathan Goforth went on to have a powerful ministry and saw revival in China and Manchuria during 1907-1909 and again in 1915 in various cities and at other times. Goforth (a Canadian) became known as China's greatest evangelist!

On the English section of the Korean website sarang.org they wrote: 'The revival of Jangdaehyun Church spread like a prairie fire to all the churches in Pyongyang, including Namsanhyun Methodist Church, then continued to sweep across the peninsula. The Holy Spirit flamed on throughout the country from January to June of 1907, leaving no place untouched.'

Church and Conversion Statistics

Statistics reveal that the revival was still going strong in 1910, though some Christians, as reported on the Christian Broadcasters Network (in the last week of June 2007) say that the Korean Revival lasted for forty years, until the Korean War (1950-1953) divided the country.

The afterglow of revival continued for a least a few years after 1910 in various towns and cities and in Jonathan Goforth's understanding, the 1903 revival, the Wonsan Revival Movement (1903-1906) had never waned or ceased, but had increased in ferocity by 1907. He wrote: 'At Tai Ku, the capital of one of the southern provinces' a ten day prayer meeting was held under the leadership of Mr Adams. 'The Holy Spirit came like a flood on the seventh day and revived them. One result was that the city church became too small, and churches sprang up all over the country. In 1905 they received 1,976 converts; in 1906 they received 3,867, and in 1907 they received 6,144.' Mr Adams said to Jonathan Goforth, "There are churches now in the country I have never seen, and some even that the evangelists have never visited!" Jonathan Goforth was told the following story of how one man, who had heard the Good News in the city of Tai Ku, took a New Testament home with him to his district and read it to his neighbours. After some time, fifty of them believed in Jesus Christ and felt it was right to form a church but they did not know how. From reading the New Testament they inferred that entrance into the church was through the door of water, by baptism. After consultation they decided that each would go home and take a bath and then meet to form their church. 'And I have no doubt that God was pleased' wrote Jonathan Goforth.

Jonathan Goforth wrote: '...By the middle of that year [1907] 'there was 30,000 converts connected to the Pyongyang centre' which flowed all over Korea. In 1907, 'there were four or five churches' so wrote Jonathan Goforth. 'The Central Presbyterian Church could hold 2,000 if the people sat close. Korean churches have no seats. The people sit on mats spread on the floor. They said in the Central Church that if you packed 2,000 in they would be so close that if anyone had to stand up a bit to ease his cramped legs he could never sit down again, for the space would just fill in.' The church had a membership of 3,000 and had been built in 1900 to accommodate 1,500 and by 1910 was the mother of eighteen churches. In 1907, the solution to the Central Church's overcrowding problem was to have separate services for women and men.[16]

South of Pyongyang, Jonathan Goforth passed through Songdo, the ancient Korean capital. In 1907 the revival had added 500 to the Church, but during a month of special meetings in 1910, 2,500 were added to the Church because of the incredible fields which were white unto harvest (John 4:35). Jonathan Goforth wrote: 'When we visited Seoul in 1907, every church was crowded. A missionary said that on a six weeks tour he had baptised 500 and recorded 700 catechumens, and that his five out-stations, in one year, had increased to twenty-five. During 1910 there were 13,000 people in Seoul who signed cards saying they wanted to become Christians, and in September of that year the Methodist churches of the city received 3,000 by baptism.

'Directly west of the capital, at the port of Chemulpo, the Methodist Mission, in 1907, had a church with 800 members. Opposite the harbour was an island with 17,000 inhabitants. The churches on the island had a baptised membership of 4,247, and more than half of them had been brought in that year. The Christians were praying that soon the whole island would become the Lords.'[17]

In the autumn of 1909, the 'Movement of Saving One Million Souls' began, where the Korean churches' aimed to win one million converts to the Lord! A worker for the British and Foreign Bible Society wrote: 'It has inspired Korean Christians with ardent zeal to propagate their faith. In no previous year has so much personal effort been made to bring a knowledge of Jesus Christ into every home in the land. On the special farthing edition of *St. Mark* in Korean our Society has issued over 600,000 copies; more than 500,000 have been bought and distributed by Korean Christians among their heathen neighbours, and these *Gospels* would be read, at a very low estimate, by considerably over one million people. Besides this the Korean Christians contributed 250,000 yen (£25,000) to the movement and *pledged to spend over 70,000 days in preaching.' *Often by those who lived off the land.

In October 1909, Dr. Chapman and Charles M. Alexander of the Chapman-Alexander Mission spent two weeks in Korea as they toured the Orient, holding meetings for missionaries and the indigenous population. A week was spent in Seoul and Alexander visited Pyongyang, noting the 'many radiant Korean Christians...where seventeen years earlier not a ray of light had brightened the darkness of heathenism,' which now 'numbered eight thousand,' whilst Chapman, due to 'serious illness' went on to Japan.[18]

In 1910, the British and Foreign Bible Society through its Bible Colporteurs sold 666,000 books to the people of Korea, most of them single *Gospels*! A Church at Sang Sim Li, which had birthed sixteen other churches in the district, in connection with the 'Million Movement' were believing for four hundred new converts; their share of the million, and so stepped out in faith and enlarged their church from 36 ft. sq. to 225 ft. sq.![19]

Jonathan Goforth wrote: 'It was clear that the revival had not died down by 1910, for in October of that year 4,000 [in Pyongyang] were baptised in one week and thousands besides sent in their names, saying they had decided to become Christians...' The Korean Presbyterians received a person publicly for Catechumen after three months and then after one year, examined them to see if they were ready for baptism, so Church members were true converts.

William Newton Blair wrote: 'In all Korea today [1910] there are no less than 250,000 Christians worshipping God in more than 2,000 places' and by 1912 there was believed to be 400,000 Christians as Mrs Louise Creigton reported.[20]

In August 1910 Korea was annexed by Japan which was the beginning of organised persecution though during this time Protestant churches grew. More than half a million migrants fled to the north of Korea.

Mrs Louise Creigton in *Missions their Rise and Development* (1912) in reference to Korea wrote: 'No country has responded more quickly to their [Christian missionary] teaching...The numbers are rapidly increasing and the Koreans show themselves not only ready hearers, but eager missionaries as soon as they learn the truth. The number of converts grows rapidly. There is one church that in a space of sixteen years has grown into five churches and yet the original congregation still numbers 2,500 and is so large that the men and women have to meet separately. The Koreans are a poor people, but already their churches are largely self-supporting and those who cannot give money give work, offering to give themselves for some fixed number of days in the year to the work of evangelist. Women have cut off their hair that it might be sold for the mission. Revival preaching [evangelistic sermons] has produced a great affect upon the Koreans, who have been won by thousands in this way. The Bible is the book which has the largest sale amongst the Korean people; they have respect for learning and the mission schools are helping much in the general spread of education and in the raising up of the native ministry. A Korean Christian speaking in 1910 of the present state of things in his country, said that the rapid conversion of the people would prove a danger unless the number of missionaries could be increased, for the people needed thorough teaching that the foundations of the Church of the future might be laid wide and deep.'[21]

By 1910 there were no less than 250,000 Christians worshipping God in more than 2,000 church buildings and a total of 950 Christian run schools, including 605 Presbyterian schools and 200 Methodist Schools which helped shape the new generation of intellectual thinking.[22]

British and Foreign Bible Society

In 1910, the year in which Japan annexed Korea, a worker for the British and Foreign Bible Society wrote: 'We recently concluded a six week tour in two south-eastern Korean provinces called North and South Chulla Do. These have a population of about two million and are occupied by the American Presbyterian Church, South. There are four mission stations, at Chunju, Kunsan, Mokpo and Kwangju, and at each centre our colporteurs are working under the superintendence of the missionaries...'

'The object of our visit was to hold classes at the various centres for our Bible-men and to accompany them on their colportage journeys. By these means we should be able to understand their needs and to give them practical as well as theoretical training for their work. As often as possible we attended the big markets that are held in the country towns. Here men gather from long distances and the Scriptures sold are carried back to isolated places never visited by the preacher. It is one of the sad features of the markets that the wine booths do a large proportion of the trade, but on the other hand it is very cheering to meet so many Christians among the crowds. As we stand in a prominent place, singing, preaching and selling, one after another will come up and help us in the service.'

At Kwangju an old blind man had found his way seventy miles to the mission hospital. For three years he had been totally blind through cataracts. After the patient had been laid on the operating table, prayer was offered and in five minutes the blind had received sight and was answering the surgeon's questions. When the old man left the ward a few days ago, he said, "Doctor, your Jesus has given me sight; I will go and preach 'the doctrine' to my friends." In this hospital, as in many others, a colporteur meets all the patients and distributes the Scriptures. Many a good work begins in far-off places through the skill of the doctor and the work of our men in their dispensaries.

'Out in the country beyond Kwangju we had the assistance of two other missionaries, so that the whole field, covering seventy square miles, might be thoroughly canvassed. During the six days over five hundred copies of the Scriptures were sold and a number of persons to whom we had preached professed conversion. Villages that previously had not heard of Christ were visited and the printed word of God was left in many homes. While many villages received us gladly, heard our message and bought our books, other districts refused to listen. Our gravest cause for concern is the widespread ignorance, indifference and callousness among Koreans...'

'At Chunju, the home of the veteran missionary and Bible translator Dr. Reynolds, profitable classes were held without colporteurs and also with a class of forty Bible-women gathered from all parts of the province. These had come as a far as seventy miles on foot, some bringing infants and all paying their own expenses; a number carried provisions of rice with them. Their sole object in coming was to study the Bible. These women are very bright and diligent students and returned after a fortnights class to their country homes and churches to impart to others the good things of Christ's kingdom.

'A Korean colporteurs life is one of real sacrifice. Some of them think nothing is too hard to endure for the cause. They trudge hundreds of miles over dreadful roads and often go hungry on their way. Starting from Mokpo, on a Sunday morning before daybreak, one Bible-man took me twenty-three miles to a little church in the midst of a needy district. My companion was one of the brightest men I have ever met, an enthusiastic, uncomplaining soul filled with the Spirit of His Master.'[23]

Paget Wilkes' Observations

Paget Wilkes, founder of the Japan Evangelistic Band visited Korea in March 1911. In his journal he wrote about the story of the Sensen Magistrate, a town in the north, where one in three of the population were Christian. When asked how things were going in his city he replied, "Go and ask the missionaries; they rule in Sensen." Paget wrote: 'He had but little to do. Quarrels and differences were settled before the Church, and not brought into the public courts – as St. Paul lays down in the Corinthians letters.'[24]

Paget Wilkes wrote that on the 26 March 1911 he 'spent a pleasant evening with Dr. Underwood, one of the oldest missionaries in Korea' who said, "Twenty-four years ago I came to Korea and there was not one protestant Christian. Today there are 200,000, i.e. one to every fifty of the population" thus making the population of Korea, 10,000,000.

The following day, Paget Wilkes was waiting on the Lord for his evening meeting, walking on the veranda of his room in the starlit night. He wrote: 'Through the darkness there reached my ears what I think is the sweetest sound I have heard in my fourteen years' sojourn in the Far East. From all parts of the city came the sound of church bells. My heart rose in praise and adoration to God for the wonder of His grace when I recalled what Dr. Underwood had told me, that in Seoul and its *immediate* neighbourhood at least 10,000 every Sunday are to be found in the house of God; while all over the city it was good to see, here and there, shops closed in observance of the Lord's Day.'[25]

Paget Wilkes recorded different points of the Korean Church that greatly impressed him and noted some observations:

1. The Holy Bible is undoubtedly the book of Korea – the love for and earnest perusal of the Scriptures is everywhere.
2. Their wonderful observance of the Lord's Day. All Christians close their shops and abstain from every kind of work.
3. The generosity of the Koreans towards God's work. Almost all the churches are self supporting and were built with Korean money.
4. The personal service and desire to spread the Gospel among the people. Many of the earlier leaders who were active in evangelism are now called upon to teach,

- 37 -

instruct and train workers, so that each member has taken up the slack.

5. The expectation and the hope (especially in the Presbyterian Church) of the coming of the Lord. The majority of the missionaries teach it plainly to the people.

2° Coming

6. There is the closest unity among all, whether Arminian or Calvinist, Presbyterian or Methodist – Canadian, Australian or American. They have real love and harmony. The only Dissenters are the High Anglicans![26]

Unity

South and North Korea

Prior to the defeat of the Japanese during World War II, leaders from China, Russia, Great Britain and the United States split the nation of Korea along the 38th parallel. Since 1945, the North has been run as a Communist state. The Korean War (1950-1953) began on the 25 June when the Communist North crossed the 38th parallel and swept down into the Democratic South causing mayhem and chaos. During this war, around 240 churches were destroyed (152 Presbyterian, 84 Methodist, 27 Holiness, 4 Salvation Army and others) and 232 Christians were either abducted (taken to North Korea) or martyred.

The Christian Council of Korea (CCK) was founded in 1989 and amongst many things, the CCK promotes revival, renewal, peaceful reunification and mission to North Korea.

By 2010, South Korea was estimated to be forty percent Christian with numerous churches having multiple services a day. South Korea is also the second largest missionary sending nation in the world with a strong economy whilst North Korea struggles to feed its own citizens.

In 1953, there were about 300,000 Christians living in North Korea. In 2009, North Korea was ranked the worst persecutor of Christians (seven years in a row) in the annual Open Doors Watch List. The regime is suspected of detaining more political and religious prisoners than any other country in the world (at least 200,000) of which 40,000-60,000 are Christian. There are a few churches in the capital, Pyongyang, but they are mainly for show, and for its citizens, owning a Bible is a crime.[27]

Please pray for North Korea – especially the Christians who are frequently tortured and executed for their faith.

Rusitu Revival (1915-1920)

In 1879, Rees Howells was born in the mining village of Brynamman, South Wales. His grandparents had been converted in the 1859 Welsh Revival and at the age of twelve, Rees left school for work at a tin mill, though he continued with evening classes. At thirteen, he became a member of the local Congregational chapel, but was unconverted.

In 1901, Rees Howells went to America to make his fortune and it was here, whilst ill, all alone in his lodgings he found the Saviour. Within a year of his near death experience he returned to the land of his fathers during the Welsh Revival (1904-1905) and got a job in a coal mine. In 1906, Rees had an incredible encounter with the Holy Spirit when he fully and unequivocally surrendered himself to Him and was led into a life of intense intercession. For a few years he was the leader of a newly founded mission, but soon he was to take a back seat as the Holy Spirit led him into the hidden life. This caused many misunderstandings, as Rees died to himself and the world, taking up his cross daily, but it was all preparation for the mission field and beyond as he saw the victories gained in intercession after intercession, including healings and conversions, as he abided in God.[1]

Over many summers from 2001-2009, I have visited Brynamman and its surrounding area and have seen many of the sites and places which were very familiar to Rees Howells, including the coal mine that he worked in, though only the Tourist Information sign points to the once bustling location which closed down years ago. His parent's house, where he grew up, (in Bryn Road), was demolished many decades ago and a bungalow has been erected in its place. But the preceding row of age-old beautiful Welsh cottages are still inhabited and give an insight into the small home that Rees was brought up in alongside his ten siblings (though a Howells' ancestral home still stands in Llandeilo Road). Bryn Road leads up to a farm and as you leave the houses behind, you close the iron gate behind you and walk across the open grass-clad Black Mountains where Rees Howells frequently roamed, spending time with the Lord as well as visiting his grandparents who looked after his invalided Uncle Dick. The wooden footbridge that Rees stood on when he made his surrender to God in 1906 (on the Black Mountains) was removed in 2008 though a single lane concrete bridge covers what was once a ford (with twin black plastic pipes). It is on the single-track A4069 / Llandeilo Road on the very edge of (though inside of) the Brecon Beacon National Park towards Gwynfe. The Brynamman meadows that Rees used to cross on the way to the mission that he founded are not as big as they used to be, due to new homes, though the public right of way across the meadow still stands.

In 1910, Rees Howells was called to live a life of faith. He resigned his position in the coal mine and began to work full time for the Lord in prayer and intercession. In December he married Elizabeth Hannah Jones whom he had known from childhood. After a short while he felt God call him into the ministry and attended the theological college of Carmarthen. After a few years they felt called to Africa and joined the South Africa General Mission (SAGM). Mrs Howells went to the Faith Mission, Edinburgh for a year of study whilst Rees Howells attended a nine month medical training course.[2]

In 1912, Samuel; Rees and Elizabeth's Howells' only child was born. In 1914, when Rees and Elizabeth were preparing for Southern Africa in their various fields of study, the toddler, Samuel, was given into the care of Rees Howells' uncle and aunt and his name was changed to Samuel Rees Howells. In July 1915, Samuel's parents left South Wales for Southern Africa. For the next five years, Rees and Elizabeth saw the hundredfold promise to those who 'give up wife, husband, child...' The story of leaving their only child behind had a deep effect on the Africans.[3]

During World War II, on the 27 January 1945, Rees Howells was preaching on 1 Kings 19:15-16 and 19-21 (Elisha being called by Elijah). Rees recalled his intercession for a Welsh village, prior to coming to Africa, which was nicknamed Hell-Fire Row, where not a single Christian lived (the village was entirely unaffected by the Welsh Revival) and the victory that he gained through his ministry to the people in that area. Rees went on to explain that as he was able to stand in the gap for a village and got the victory, then he would be able to do it for a district or a country. Secondly, because he loved the village then he could love the world. Rees said, "I was called to the ministry and afterwards to Africa, and those souls in Africa became more to me than my life...Could anything be greater than to go out to the heathen with the Risen Christ. I knew what He could do in the village – as a proof, that call was the greatest thing, it was greater than Samuel [his son]." Rees then went on to explain that Samuel would have to be put on the altar, just as Isaac was, but in doing so, he was able to claim 10,000 souls for Christ. Rees said, "I went to Africa and oh, the love I had for those natives, and in two months the revival came – I knew I would have 10,000 souls for Samuel..."

In 1936, Miss Eva Stuart Watt, Home Secretary of the Sudan United Mission, was confronted by the estimate that fifteen hundred million of the world's people were unevangelised, but it was just a figure on paper until the Lord reminded her of the word of His servant, Rees Howells who said, "Blood is thicker than water, and you have to love your own, made dear to you by the ties of blood. Now let Spirit be thicker than blood, and love souls because Jesus loves them – love them as if they were your own flesh and blood." '4

Rees and Elizabeth Howells, arrived on African soil in late August 1915, they were situated in the Rusitu Valley (also known as Rossitu outside a town called Chipinge), Gazaland, (then Southern Rhodesia and now modern day Zimbabwe), near the border of Portuguese East Africa (modern day Mozambique) and worked under the SAGM alongside Mr and Mrs Hatch. Their fellow missionaries knew they had come from the land of revivals and asked them if they had brought the blessing with them. Rees told them, that the source of all revival is the Holy Ghost, and that He could do among them what He had done in Wales! Rees was asked to preach on 'revival,' but as there had been no revival in that part of the country he used the word 'Pentecost.'

Within six weeks, preaching via a translator, the Holy Spirit began to move upon the Christians. Rees said, "As I preached on revival and what God had prophesised through Joel, I came to believe and expect it."

On Friday 1 October 1915, as a dozen or so Christians met at the home of the Howells' at the Rusitu mission station, Elizabeth taught them the chorus, 'Lord, send a revival, and let it begin in me,' which caught on and was sung throughout the working week. Within a week, on Thursday the seventh, the four missionaries of the Rusitu station met together for evening prayer for revival. After a period of time, the Lord assured Rees Howells that their prayers were heard and that Pentecost was coming to their district. He told them to rise from their knees – they had the assurance of victory. Rees said, "People had worked on that mission station for seven years without a single convert. They had laid a wonderful foundation but when the Holy Spirit came, He swept hundred into the Kingdom."

On Sunday 10 October 1915 (Rees Howells' birthday), revival came, though the Holy Spirit revealed it to Rees on the ninth that revival was coming the following day![5] Rees said, "...As I preached in the morning you could feel the Spirit coming on the congregation. In the evening down He came. I shall never forget it. He came upon a young girl, Kufase by name who had fasted for three days under conviction that she was not ready for the Lord's coming. As she prayed she broke down crying, and within five minutes the whole congregation were on their faces crying to God. Like lighting and thunder the power came down. I had never seen this even in the Welsh Revival. I had only heard about it with [Charles] Finney and others. Heaven had opened, and there was no room to contain the blessing. I lost myself in the Spirit and prayed as much as they did." The meeting went on late into the night. Rees wrote: 'You can never describe those meetings when the Holy Spirit comes down. I shall never forget the sound in the district that night – praying in every kraal [village huts].'[6]

The next day the Holy Spirit came again and people were on their knees until 6pm. For six days there was prayer, confession of sin and testimonies (often twenty-five people would be on their feet at once) until nearly all the Rusitu Christians were right with God. For the next fifteen months there would be two revival meetings a day, without a single break, meetings all day on Friday and the Howells' were trying to learn the local language, Chindau. Hundreds were converted and as the news of the revival spread, other mission stations were affected, beginning at Mount Silinda, where one man confessed to murder. Mr Hatch and Rees Howells travelled to Mount Silinda with three Rusitu Christians and on that day 'about a hundred souls came to complete deliverance and victory, and on the Saturday scores came through into the new life of peace and surrender, and instead of soul agony, the majority were praising and singing with joy.' The next day, 'over two hundred had come into liberty.'

After fifteen months, the head office of the SAGM in Cape Town, inspired by the Rusitu Revival, requested all the brethren at their mission stations to spend thirty minutes each morning in prayer for revival, beginning at 7am. After about one month, Rees Howells, after pleading the promise of Malachi 3:10 (the open windows from heaven), in the spirit saw revival descending on every mission station and for a whole week was in the glory![7]

In early 1917, forty-three SAGM missionaries, representatives from nearly all the SAGM twenty-five mission stations met for a three week conference at Durban, South Africa. Rees Howells was asked to preach, the Holy Spirit came and for three weeks the missionaries were in the midst of revival, being searched by the Spirit of Grace. On the 28 January 1945, Rees preached from John 20:19-23 – Jesus appearing to the disciples; He breathed on them and they received the Holy Spirit. Rees then recalled the events at Durban in 1917 and said, "...There were two from every mission station meeting together for three weeks. I remember the first meeting, I went through all that the Holy Ghost had done and the revival we had. When you relate what has happened, there is the same effect as when it comes – like Paul before Agrippa [Acts 26] you can never preach to missionaries or ministers. I told them, when I went to Rusitu, I took in me the source of all revivals [the Holy Spirit living in a fully surrendered vessel]...As I was telling them, the forty-three missionaries and others, all went down on their knees and they all prayed for the Holy Ghost. I preached that the condition of the Holy Ghost coming is that you give up your will. Your will and the will of the Holy Spirit will never live together, and I told them, if they were willing, the Holy Ghost was more [than] ready to come in and bless them...In Durban, it happened on the Monday again [the following day] and the missionaries asked to leave all the business until they had the blessing...Those forty-three missionaries were representing thousands of natives and they knew with the power they had before, they were failures, and they knew the Holy Ghost had come. The Holy Ghost came down on every meeting of those three weeks and every missionary was a changed person...everyone came free!"

Under the SAGM, Rees Howells was commissioned to travel to all the SAGM mission stations in Southern Africa for six months, which was extended to two years – so the Rusitu Revival flowed into the Gazaland Revival. He also travelled to the countries of Swaziland, Pondoland, Bomvanaland, Tembuland and Zululand, (Southern Africa) over 11,000 miles and saw revival in every mission station! Rees and his colleague Medhill, at Mbabane assured the missionaries that 'in every way it was like the Welsh Revival' of 1904-1905 and said that 'the power in the meeting was indescribable.' 'Renewal of life was also reported from Christian communities in Natal.'[8]

In late 1919, Rees and Elizabeth Howells returned to the Rusitu mission station and found that the revival was still continuing, though hardly any of the married men were converted. This was put down to Labola, the custom in which a father would sell his daughter in marriage and therefore the financial incentives of Labola made the native married men shun Christianity with its financial loses. Within a short space of time, five of Rees' workmen were saved. After World War I (1914-1918) Influenza (Spanish flu) swept the world as troops returned home after the war (it has been estimated that ten percent of the world's population died at that time). When it reached the Rusitu station, the heathen said that it was because the ancestral spirits had been offended by the breaking of Labola. Rees had the assurance of the Holy Spirit that it was a blessing in disguise (Romans 8:28) and had been told by Him that no one on his mission station would die! This he told to the local chief, who confessed that his witchdoctors were unable to help and that two of them were the first to die!

The Lord gave Rees Howells great wisdom and told him to turn the chapel into a hospital and to put fires in at night, so as to keep the temperature even. Soon, fifty people were ill and some were very serious. As word spread, (within a twenty miles radius) that death could not be found on Rusitu mission station; the natives flocked there and 'conviction of sin took hold of many' and they were converted. After the epidemic was over, one whole side of the chapel was filled with converted married men![9]

In Christmas 1920, Rees and Elizabeth Howells returned to Britain on furlough and they resigned from the mission in 1922. In 1924, as led by the Lord, they founded the Bible College of Wales (BCW) and later a school for missionary children in Swansea, South Wales. BCW saw its last graduation in 2009.

In the early 1980s, Rhodesian born Michael Howard visited the Rusitu Valley and the site of the destroyed Rusitu mission station. With his team of intercessors and evangelists they held a crusade where many hundreds came the first night and it soon 'swelled into thousands.' Michael Howard wrote: 'Multitudes were getting saved and many [were] healed from diverse sickness and diseases.' The last two days of the campaign were most powerful. Michael wrote: 'I saw His power come down in such reality that one and another native was picked off the ground and seemed suspended in mid-air...Heaven came down and saturated us all.'[10]

Budapest, Hungary (1937-1938)

I first came across this revival in Hungary after reading a fleeting reference by J. Edwin Orr, who noted: 'The stirring revival in Budapest...under James Stewart, who preaches all over Europe by interpretation.'[1]

Scottish evangelist, James A. Stewart of Glasgow (known as Jimmie to his friends) had seen revival in and around Riga, Latvia for six months during 1931-1932; he saw revival in Prague, and others parts of Czech-Slovakia from September 1936 to March 1937. He saw revival in Budapest, and other parts of Hungary for seven weeks during 1937-1938, when he held two evangelistic campaigns 'during which thousands packed the great auditorium each night and the city was swept with revival.'[2]

In 1931, nineteen-year-old James Stewart, after preaching up and down England, received his call to Eastern Europe. He first landed at Riga, Latvia, where he met Pastor William Fetler, the founder of the Russian Missionary Society. William Fetler translated for him in the winter of 1931 and then James Stewart went on through Poland and up into the Carpathian mountain range and farther south.[3]

Pastor William Fetler was known as the "Apostle to Russia" after his banishment from Russian soil in 1914. Before his exile, he had planted a dozen preaching centres in St. Petersburg, others in Moscow and the two thousand-seat "Dom Evangelia" in Petrograd, the largest evangelical church in the Russian empire. In Riga, Latvia, William Felter had also built the Salvation Temple, the biggest church in Riga.[4]

At the beginning of the twentieth century, an Intervarsity student, Aladar Szabo was so concerned about the state of his country, Hungary, that he made his view known to his colleagues in the Theological Academy of the Reformed Church in Sárospatak. He was expelled on the charge of 'introducing sectarianism.' After his ordination, Rev. Szabo began to preach the pure truths of the Gospel, formed young men's Christian associations and an evangelistic movement known as 'Bethania.' From 1905, these groups 'rapidly multiplied all over the country.' Beginning in around 1932, young Reformed ministers allied with Bethania, started systematic evangelistic campaigns, for a minimum of ten days duration, anywhere they were invited. Other Christian agencies soon caught inspiration from the Bethania workers conferences.

Soon, 'the spirit of prayer for revival...began to pervade the Evangelical Alliance of Hungary, an interdenominational Christian union with its headquarters in Budapest. In 1936, two representatives of the Keswick Council visited them. The following May, Rev. E. L. Langston followed their efforts with a six day conference, which was 'a very blessed time...There were signs then that a revival was on its way.'

In late 1937, the president of the Evangelical Alliance, Dr. Csia, invited James Stewart for an extended evangelistic campaign. When Stewart arrived in Budapest, 'he was simple in dress and appearance' so wrote Professor Kiss of the Budapest University. Looking back on what happened, he wrote: 'We had little faith that anything would happen...It became evident that our prayer-life was poor, and our sacrifice and obedience only partial.' Recalling the revival he wrote: 'Nobody has ever seen in this generation...such workings of the Holy Spirit as at this time. The most influential men and women of our nation have come under the sound of the Gospel.'

In late November 1937, James Stewart left Sofia, Bulgaria, and arrived in Budapest for a four week campaign (ending just before Christmas 1937), which he would recommence in March 1938 with additional help. The meetings began in a German Methodist Church and the second week was given over to evangelism. Numbers increased so they moved into one of the largest Calvinistic churches in the city. About, 2,500 'packed the building...that one evening three successive meetings had to be held to relieve the crush!' But the police cancelled all further meetings and gave Stewart notice to leave the country. The Christians began to pray and the Prime Minister of Hungary 'personally gave instructions to the Chief of Police that he must in no way hinder the campaign!'

On the third week, a great concert hall was hired, the famous four thousand-seat Vigado on the Danube River. The Christians let go of their differences and came together as one to seek His face. 'As many as 2,500 would meet solely to pray. Hundreds, who had only heard of prayer during times of revival, knew it experimentally in their lives and their own beloved country. They seemed to be praying all day long. It was one sob and one agonising cry to the Father to save their friends and their city and their nation.' Special days were set apart for prayer and fasting. During the day, James Stewart systematically visited the schools and colleges and every evening, before the main meeting, he would hold youth gatherings, address their issues, and the youth knew how to pray under 'the mighty convicting power of God, the Holy Spirit.'

In the main meetings were the educated professors and leading businessmen of the city as well as students and country peasants in their sheep-skin coats, with old ladies with black shawls thrown over their shoulders. Protestants, Catholics, Jew and infidels sat side by side as James Stewart, with a good sense of humour, preached a practical Gospel from the Bible.

In 1939, Eva Stuart Watt, alongside James Stewart and his wife, Ruth, revisited the scenes of former glory and wrote: 'During these meetings many hundreds of backsliders were restored, and hundreds more found the peace of sins forgiven.' One evening a pale faced psychologist, one of the most eminent in Hungary, came up to the platform and made an announcement through the megaphone. He confessed that he had been making money by deceiving his patients and he asked their (the audiences) forgiveness. He wrote to James Stewart afterwards: '...I have lived a proud and presumptuous life. I trusted in my own righteousness and boasted in my scientific attainments. But there was sin in my life. Coming to your meetings, the word of God pierced my soul night after night. My sin rose before me like a mountain. I had to make that confession before God and before man about my false methods with my patients; and by His grace I am making restitution.'

The fourth week was given over to Bible study, to ground the new converts in the faith. 'On the closing evening the glory of the Lord filled the place, so that James [Stewart] could not preach. The whole audience just wept in the presence of God.'[5]

In between the first and second evangelistic campaigns, James Stewart was invited to Dublin, Northern Ireland to give a week of lectures on the subject of revival, but it was also a time for a welcome rest. The special meetings "A Back-to-God Campaign" began on Saturday the 26 February 1938. It was held in the Metropolitan Hall and 'the hush and solemnity of eternity pervaded all the meetings.'

Eva Stuart Watt wrote: 'The afternoon talks to Christians upstairs were times when the dew of heaven dropped on parched ground; and by the end of the week we had to move into a larger hall. The prayer meetings that started with half a dozen or so soon grew in numbers and intensity till the room was overflowing. The local papers gave full publicity to the meetings; and Catholics as well as Protestants were drawn together to fill up the body of that great building, where Moody and Sankey, and Torrey and Alexander, witnessed such a work of grace in the last generation. Revival had not yet come, but there was a conviction of sin among God's people.'[6]

In March 1938, James Stewart was joined by his younger brother, Douglas and Dr. and Mrs R. E. Neighbour from America for a second campaign in Budapest, lasting three weeks, running into April. They were met with opposition and had difficulty in obtaining a suitable building. Eventually they hired an exhibition hall, the "Tattersol," a gigantic unheated high-roofed shed with sand floor. In the daytime, it was used as a riding school and for cattle shows!

The weather was against them, the Danube River was frozen over. James Stewart got a dose of influenza, but rose from his bed each evening to preach. Conditions were so severe that there was talk of stopping the campaign until a warmer spell. Thousands of chairs were laid out and the people came. The Christians prayed for better weather and the next few days saw a decided increase in spring sunshine; 3,000 to 4,000 turned up on week days with 5,000 on Sunday, 'causing a stir in the city and giving the meetings considerable prominence in the press.' Douglas Stewart helped his brother James with the young people. Universities, colleges, schools and several youth organisations came into contingent and on the final Sunday afternoon, upwards of 5,000 met for a farewell service.

Prayer hallmarked both campaigns in Budapest, which flowed over into revival. 'As the tide of prayer rose, the tide of blessing rose with it. When Christians humbled themselves and confessed their sin, sinners came under conviction. Hundreds of people gathered all over the city of Budapest without a leader from 7am and intermittently through the day, to call upon God.'

The Methodist Conference Annual Report of May 1938 wrote: '...It is clear that his testimony was received by crowds of a size hitherto unknown in our little country. As many as four thousand would crowd into his meetings; and not only in the capital, but everywhere in the largest towns, thousands flocked to hear him. And this surely was not the outcome of widespread advertisement alone, but a proof of the hunger of the people after the true Gospel. It was a testimony of the living Saviour, who works today and with whom one can have a vital experience.'[7] See Appendix C for more on the life of James A. Stewart.

Congo Revival (1953-1957)

The Congo Revival (1953-1957) was documented[1] by eight senior unnamed Worldwide Evangelisation Crusade (WEC) missionaries at six main mission stations, Lubutu, Opienge, Wamba, Ibambi, Egbita and Malingwia in the North Eastern, Belgian Congo (modern day Democratic Republic of Congo, formerly known as Zaire). The WEC with their ten mission stations worked in an area of some four hundred miles long and two hundred and fifty miles at its broadest point, which had been gradually occupied since 1913/14 under C. T. Studd.

The East African Revival (1930s-1950s) had it beginnings in the revival which began in Uganda in 1936 and by 1937 was widespread across the country in various locations. Uganda was the central hub of the East African wheel of revival which touched Kenya, Tanganyika (modern day Tanzania), Belgian Ruanda (now Rwanda and Burundi), the Belgian Congo and the Sudan so noted Max Warren whom Bishop Oliver Allison of the Sudan called a 'Missionary Statesman and Prophet.'[2] But from the accounts of the missionaries who were used in the Congo Revival (1953-1957) there appears to be no direct link with the East African Revival. Ivor Davies, who was a missionary at Opinege, North Eastern Belgian Congo, stated that at his mission station he had 'told the natives of the Ruanda blessing and also of that in Korea, so that much prayer had gone up for the work.' Revival broke out at his mission station in May 1953, whereas at Lubutu, the revival broke out in February 1953 which was the beginning of the Congo Revival.[3]

The revival fires began in the Congo when the missionaries and the natives decided to get right with God. There was much heart and soul searching, prayer and teaching on the Holy Spirit for months prior to the outbreak of revival. For years, I was unsure of how long this revival continued as no book had ever recorded it but in early October 2006 I had the opportunity of speaking to the Rev. David Morgan Davies and his wife Anne Elizabeth Davies, (aged 97 and 96 respectively) at their home in South Wales, UK. They were the head missionaries at Wamba mission station, which consisted of the populous Mabudu tribe during the Congo Revival, and they told me that it had ended in 1957. David had begun training at the Bible College of Wales under Rees Howells in October 1930.

The Congo Revival began at Lubutu in February 1953 and within five months had spread to all the WEC mission stations, outstations and to two other mission agency stations when they requested 'revival teams' to visit them. The revival largely moved by extension when fire carriers, those who had been revived, took the holy fire with them to another location. As they preached or shared their testimonies, the Holy Spirit would descend on the mission compound and touch Christians and heathen alike, bringing them into a correct relationship with the living God, through His Son, Jesus Christ and bringing them into the fullness of the Holy Spirit. God demands that we live to glorify Him. We are called to be holy (1 Peter 1:16) because without holiness we cannot see the Lord (Hebrews 12:14) So the revival (as in all revivals) was about cleaning up Christians (being revived, renewed and transformed) and converting the heathen to a saving knowledge of Jesus Christ as there is no other name under heaven by which we must be saved.

At one mission station, they thought a hurricane was coming as the wind of the Spirit blew through the building and came upon many. Numerous shy native ladies would shout praises, "Hallelujah!" at the top of the voices. Others shook all over and collapsed on the floor in groans and travail as intercession for souls was birthed in them, whilst others groaned and writhed under conviction of sin. Some people in different mission stations saw holy light or a bright light as part of a vision. People were slain in the meetings and would tremble and jerk uncontrollably or perspire and fall off their seat and roll in the mud in agony of soul. At first some of the missionaries were naturally hesitant about these manifestations – were they from God or not? But as people came through to victory and testified of their sin in front of all, knowing that they had been pardoned by God through the shed blood of Jesus Christ, the uncertain missionaries knew it to be a genuine heaven-sent revival.

Some in the meetings would try to imitate the manifestations of the Spirit as seen upon other persons, whether by shaking, jerking or just getting over-excited in the flesh, trying to 'work up' the blessing. One flaky person claimed to be the Holy Spirit and was sharply rebuked, but the people had a teachable spirit and were able to receive correction from those in leadership. The elders, missionaries or those in charge of the meetings rebuked those who were in the flesh and instructed accordingly as there is a difference between hindering the Spirit and working with the Spirit. Those with positions of authority who negate their responsibility which has been entrusted to them, to exhort and to correct in the spirit of meekness and humility, thereby sin and grieve the Holy Spirit when they fail to do their duty. Also, other mentally disturbed people were set free from demons, by the power of God, in the name of Jesus Christ.

A senior missionary wrote: 'Grieve not the Spirit. Criticism, or attributing to the flesh that which is of the Spirit, can hinder revival tremendously; let us not be guilty of either.'[4]

Singing and prayer went on into the early hours in all of the mission stations as the brethren had such thankful spirits that they had been saved and forgiven. Some people hardened their hearts and refused to confess their sin and turn from their wicked ways. Some of these heathen held onto trees and posts to stop them from being thrown to the ground by the Holy Spirit, but He always got His way! Even Christians were literally flung to the ground by the Spirit of God! People's hands and knees were fused together; others were stuck to the ground and would not be released until they had confessed their sin!

Several of the missionaries commented, that a lot of what they saw could have been straight out of John Wesley's *Journal*. Even 'good living,' soul winning Christians came under the conviction of their secret sin, which had to be brought to light. Confessions of adultery, lust, robbery etc. were common place from the front of the church, those who had been there before used to encourage the confessor to confess all in the sight of God and his or her brethren (James 5:16). It was a humbling time for hundreds of people.

The Holy Spirit had given life to that which had been dead and the church became alive, a living reality; healings took place, singing and praying in tongues resounded. The natives sung like never before and in several of the mission stations construction work which had carried on for weeks or months was completed in a matter of days as the workers did an honest days work. There was much restitution and things made right. Some of the natives, who owned orchards of special palm trees from which palm wine were obtained, upon conversion or under conviction of their use, cut them down at great financial loss to themselves as a new life in Christ and the selling of alcohol (and even indirect selling, from leasing out a wine palm plantation) were incompatible.

In August 1990, David Davies gave some of the highlights of his time in the Belgian Congo / Zaire over a period of 27 years. He wrote: 'Time would fail me to tell of the mighty visitation of the Spirit of God to the whole area where WEC related churches were planted The revival covered an expanse as large as the UK, touching mission station and churches hundreds of miles apart. How the Lord Jesus was exalted. How the people loved one another; loved the Bible studies, the prayer meetings and evangelising the pagans. And what wonderful conversions!'[5]

Norman Grubb in *The Liberating Secret* (1955) in the context of the Congo revival wrote: '[In revival] the veil between heaven and earth grows thin...the fountains of the great deep are broken up, and normal restraints and respectabilities are forgotten...'

'Who can say how these things happened? The Gospel has been preached with utmost faithfulness for forty years among many thousands in this area of about 400 miles by 250. Now the Lord, whom they sought, has suddenly come to His temple, like a refiner's fire, and like fullers soap. How continually have the missionaries mourned over the many to whom the Gospel was not real. They heard, they professed, they repented (or appeared to), but they didn't get born again with the new birth which changes everything. There were the saints and the soldiers, thank God, the real ones, but they were the exception! But now! Who may abide the day of His coming? The missionaries could hardly stand it. Was it real, or was it counterfeit? The noise, the confusion, the terrific weeping, the people struck down as if dead. Could this be the God of order? No, it was not as yet; it was the exposure of satanic disorder in lives which had to be cleaned up before that blessed Dove could reign in His order and quietness.

'At first some of the missionaries tried to stop it, running hither and thither to try and quieten the people. Thank God they were restrained of the Spirit, for when they saw that hidden sins were coming out which wild horses could not have dragged out by natural means, often husband before wife, or wife before husband, yet each so occupied with getting their own lives right, that they had no time for the other; when they saw restitution of long stolen goods, resentments and criticism wept over as much as gross sins, men falling on the necks of men, and women on women in reconciliation, the missionaries often being besieged with those who had apologies to make; when they saw these things, they knew it was of God. Like a flame, it leapt from district to district, usually through the testimony of some revived African.'

Norman Grubb then went on to share how the missionaries soon found issues in their own lives which had to be dealt with, which brought them side by side in repentance with their African brethren, and wrote about some of the physical phenomena. 'Emotional we say? Who cares, when it is evidently the mighty working of God...God has come. It was like an electric current running through the congregation, but it was a moral current, not just an emotional one, or the missionaries would have rejected it at once. It brought Jesus in the midst, first in awful holiness, then in abounding grace...There were some physical healings, not many, for it was not a particular part of the message. But when God draws near, anything happens to soul and body...'[6]

Ibambi mission station (also spelt Imbai) had a history of revival. Revival first broke out in 1925 under C. T. Studd, the pioneering missionary; again, on New Year's Eve 1934 which lasted one week (into January 1935) under the Roberts' siblings (Jack, Lily and Ivy). The third move of God was when the Holy Spirit came and a deeper work of revival was witnessed for eleven weeks during 1935-1936 under Lily and Ivy Roberts just prior to the closure of the mission station. The Belgian government had limited the number of European mission stations.[7]

In 1953, the leader of Ibambi (the mission station having been re-opened) and his wife wrote: 'The Holy Ghost came down in mighty power. We have never seen anything like it before. Words fail to describe it, but we know something now of what it must have been like on the day of Pentecost. As one prayed, another began to pray, and another, and then the whole congregation together. Such a noise as they poured out their souls in prayer and praise to God. Men, women, boys and girls just drunk with the Spirit, many shaking beyond their control, others throwing themselves on the floor, some leaning, some standing...We just stood there amazed, but were not afraid, as we knew it was the Spirit working...It was impossible to makes oneself heard. If this had not been of God, it would have been terrible, as they were beyond all human control.

'Strange things have accompanied every true revival, but when the Spirit is allowed full sway He is able to take care of His own work. We need to be ready for any revelation He gives. As the enemy seeks to get in, we shall have discernment and be able to recognise his devices. We have certainly seen manifestations we never saw before, but we know the work is of the Spirit because of the outworking of it in a practical way in so many lives.

'The Holy Spirit leads the meeting and we don't know what is going to happen next. We are so full of joy that God has visited us at last. He has no set way of working, and it seems to come differently in each place.'[8]

Sometime in 1953, (the exact month is not recorded) the Holy Spirit descended on the 'hard and dry district' amongst the Meje tribe; where missionaries had toiled for more than twenty years at the Egbita Centre. An evangelist who was taking the teacher training course at Egbita saw his son, a toddler, born with a dislocated hip, healed after a few days, after the boy had received prayer. A missionary at Egbita wrote: 'God has done in a few days things we had never seen in twenty years of labour, but one realises too that nothing has been lost of all the efforts of sowing and reaping. It is as though the Lord has reaped in a day.'

There were numerous conversions and the missionaries were nearly pulled to the ground by so many natives desiring to confess their sins and to ask forgiveness for all sorts of grievances! The missionary continued: 'The Spirit has hit hard on the pastors, evangelists and elders for being below standard with only selfish motives. It is true the dry bones can live, hallelujah!'[9]

One missionary wrote: 'We are convinced that wherever there is a genuine desire for revival and a willingness to accept what God sends, without any heart reservations, God will not pass them by. Let us humbly, by prayer and heart searching, seek God's face continually and be ready to pay the price for revival.'[10]

Signs and Fruit of the Congo Revival
During the Congo Revival, there were distinct signs, fruit and effects of the revival. Theses were:

1. Major conviction of sin, public confession of sins, asking forgiveness for wrongs (by people and leaders alike) and restitution of even the smallest items or debts.
2. Often those who were under deep conviction would shake, tremble, collapse on the floor (even be thrown to the floor) and writhe in agony or perspire profusely until they had confessed their sins and got right with God.
3. Those who had been saved and forgiven had a really thankful spirit and this was often expressed in song.

4. There was much emphasis on the shed blood of Jesus and a living reality of the fullness of the Spirit.
5. The native women also opened up in singing. Great boldness came on many of them whom were previously shy and retiring (this was probably a culture trait which had been broken).
6. There was a teachable spirit. Christians who moved from the Spirit into the flesh, those who tried to 'work up' the blessing or who stepped out of line would happily receive correction from those in leadership and change their ways immediately.
7. The Christians were burdened (intercession) for the unconverted and those under conviction of sin so they could be saved and brought into a correct relationship with Jesus Christ.

The Test of a Transformed Life

Within a few days of the revival commencing at the Opienge mission station, Ivor Davies, the senior missionary (his younger brother Rev. David Davies was the senior missionary at Wamba) heard so many confessions of sin that he felt it necessary to challenge those had had stolen to make restitution and there was a steady response. During the next week he put forth the following tests as a frame of reference to those who claimed to be changed persons:
1. Is there love for the truth and are you sensitive to it?
2. What is your attitude to a lie? Is it hateful to you?
3. Are you willing as far as possible, to put a wrong right by making restitution or asking forgiveness for the person wronged.
4. Are you willing to make a public confession of the Lord Jesus?
5. Does the praise go to the Lord?[11]

Children in Revival

Revival broke out at the Opienge mission station in May 1953, 'as a tornado of blessing.' At one of the meetings within the first week of the visitation of the Holy Spirit, Ivor Davies recalling the event wrote: 'The girls from school were present and the Lord began a mighty work among them. The schoolboys, except for two or three were not touched. But the following Saturday an elder, marched down the aisles, first praising the Lord and then urging all to repent. Men, women, boys and girls were overcome by the power of the Spirit.'[12]

Revival broke out at the Wamba mission station on Sunday 19 July 1953 and both the kindergarten (a preschool for children ages 4-6 to prepare them for primary school) and the schoolboys and schoolgirls were affected by the move of God as well as all those on the mission station. In the first evening service of the revival, the whole compound was ablaze and 'hardly anyone slept all night' so wrote David Davies. 'Those who were blessed broke forth into singing from time to time. Others groaned and cried under conviction of sin. There was a lot of crying among the school children, especially the girls...'

'On Tuesday morning, the Spirit of God came down on the girls...There were the cryings and wailing and sobbing out of their sins.' The women were called to help the girls and they did what they could to lead the children through to salvation. 'After a couple of hours most of the girls had come through to peace...We tried putting them to school, but it was really hopeless; some were too full of joy to come back to earth and others too burdened about their sins to pay attention to schooling. Cries of agony and songs of praise kept breaking out all day.'

In the evening, David Davies and fellow associates went across to the boys' compound. He wrote: 'What a sight! Boys in groups dealing with their fellows, some lying on the ground, others on their knees and yet others dancing and singing for sheer joy.'

On Wednesday morning, the kindergarten was visited by the Holy Spirit! Anne Davies wrote: 'The Holy Spirit came upon the children during their morning prayer. Some of the houseboys and workmen ran to the school and became personal workers on the spot.'

On Thursday, teacher Gbadi came through and received the blessing after earlier rolling in the red mud, agonising over his sins. Eventually, after loudly confessing his sins mingled with cries for God's mercy he became free – 'a new creature in Christ, but he was of no use in the schoolroom for a few days' so wrote David Davies. 'Instead of teaching the children, he would be delving into the New Testament or hymnal and simply could not bring himself sufficiently down to earth to teach class.'[13]

Revival broke out in Bomili area in the summer of 1953 – the exact month is not specified, but at its commencement 800 people were present for a weekend conference as two missionaries from Opienge visited. Spiritually speaking, they brought hot coals from the altar to set Bomili ablaze for God's glory.

One of the lady missionaries had been much burdened for the schoolgirls throughout the term. One night, a few weeks before the commencement of revival, she was endued with power from on high as she rededicated herself to God's service, after being burdened for the schoolgirls' souls. The revival broke out a few days before the end of term and touched the schoolgirls at the farewell meeting which had been arranged by the burdened lady missionary. She wrote: 'Many confessed to sin of one form or another, such as little unrighteous acts, which had meant nothing to them until Spirit of God had convicted them.' The missionary felt charged with power as the Holy Spirit came upon her and she let out 'bursts of hallelujah' which were echoed by the schoolchildren. 'Soon the compound was ringing with their cries, as the Spirit came down in convicting power and confessions of deep sin were made. This went on until about midnight. Yes, revival has come!'[14]

At Ibambi mission station, (the headquarters of the WEC mission) revival broke out when the field leader returned to Ibambi and gave testimony to what he had seen and heard at another mission station. Later, as they began to pray, the Holy Spirit descended on the entire congregation and 'bedlam broke loose.' People 'were stretched out all over the floor screaming out their sins. They just fell...' so wrote a missionary. 'Day and night, God dealt with 400 people on the station.'

The schoolboys came asking for special prayer before leaving for their month off, as it was one of the holidays. The 220 boys were concerned that they would be overcome by temptation when they returned home to their respective pagan villages and families. They were told that 'if God had really met with them and filled them with His Holy Spirit, they would be able to stand against all temptation.' A month later, 220 schoolboys returned 'still praising the Lord' and had brought thirty new students with them. Around the campfire that night the missionaries were told of the 'hundreds of souls who had come to the Lord through them. This was also true of the girls on the station.' On Sunday lunchtime, some boys in their early teens felt led to fast and pray for the new students whom they had brought back with them and were located in the prayer room that was set aside for the boys. By suppertime they were still praying.[15]

Central Bible School

The converts from across the Belgian Congo that were deemed the most promising were always sent to the Central Bible School at Ibambi and were trained as evangelists before returning to some of the larger churches, whilst a few were elected by the churches as pastors – men of spiritual maturity who also had an itinerant ministry. Married couples were also sent to the Bible School.

The revival came to Ibambi in July 1953 in 'three distinct waves.' Firstly upon the station people and the schools and then secondly, a few weeks later the Holy Spirit came upon the Central Bible School. When the fire fell at Ibambi the Bible students were out on a trek, but news travels fast. Some had already made up their minds that they had nothing to confess, whilst others arrived back at base with 'fear and tremblings for the Holy Spirit had already begun His work of convicting of sins.' The third wave was when the local evangelists and out-church leaders returned to base for a conference.

In the first fellowship meeting (the second wave of blessing) when the students were intermingled with the crowds, the Holy Spirit singled the students out (the others had been dealt with when the Holy Spirit first came), one woman was on her knees weeping, whilst a man was confessing his sins to God. 'During the next few days, God dealt with each student in turn.' One woman, as she was confessing her hatred in her heart towards others was thrown to the cement floor by the Holy Spirit. A she rose to her feet, joy flooded her soul. Early one morning the missionaries were awoken 'by terrible sobbing' from a Bible student. He came 'for prayer to be delivered from a temper which had been a detriment in his service to the Lord. He sobbed his way to glorious victory.'

A missionary wrote: 'One could multiply stories of restitutions which had to be made, incompatibility between husbands and wives, neglect of quite times etc. When all were through, we had a real baptism of joy; the whole station heard and many came around to see what was happening. It was joy unspeakable and full of glory. We had a new Bible School; head knowledge was now becoming heart experience; songs of praise arose to the throne day and night. We seemed to be wrapped around the very presence of the Lord. It seemed but a step to reach the glory. Prayer sessions were now alive with power, concern for loved ones, backsliders and pagans. What a volume of prayer ascended, mingled with tears, as they poured out their hearts to the Lord, some on their knees, others prostrate.'

At the WEC's northernmost station at Malingwia among the Ababua tribe, many of the husbands and wives had got through together; repentance, renouncing and forsaking their sins followed by the fullness of the Spirit. After two weeks of revival many of the married couples felt 'a definite call of God' to some needy place and testified as such. Then young couples, who were 'mostly former schoolchildren now married with the beginnings of families, came out saying God had called [them] to Bible School.'[16]

Missionaries and a Revivalist's Testimony

I was present at a Bible College meeting when the Rev. David Davies was the guest speaker and shared his experiences during the Congo Revival. David and his wife Anne were head missionaries at Wamba mission station, which consisted of the populous Mabudu tribe. One of the things that I distinctly remember from that meeting was that during the revival; the locals returned hundreds of stolen shovels and other tools to their foreman, as after each portion of construction work prior to this move of God they used to keep them for themselves!

Rev. David Davies also stated that during World War II (1939-1945) out on the mission field in the heart of Africa, the missionaries were unaware of how the war was going, until it ended; only to discover that the post office had kept a room full of his mail which was for five years undeliverable!

At the end of the meeting there was opportunity to ask him questions and there were many. The meeting lasted thirty minutes beyond the usual ninety minutes service, especially considering there were thirteen meetings a week (one each morning and one each evening except Saturday) and this was on Friday evening after a hard week of lectures. One person asked, "How do you justify people falling over [in the revival]?" "Well" he replied, "At first my brother and I were a bit sceptical about it, but knew that if we could get a precedent in Scripture then it would be safe to assume that it was from God. We found Revelation 6:17 '...who shall be able to stand [in His presence].' Well that was good enough for us!" In my mind I can still see (and hear) the Rev. Davies behind the pulpit, stating what he had witnessed and what had happened to him nearly fifty years ago in the middle of Africa – it was still very vivid in his mind and evident in his close walk with the Lord.

In early October 2006, I had the opportunity and privilege of speaking to the Rev. David Davies and his wife Anne Elizabeth, at their fixed caravan home in South Wales, UK. Both David and Anne had been born in 1910, with just six months separating them. In 1930, David began his studies at The Bible College of Wales (BCW); which lasted for three years, whilst his older brother Ivor Davies was already a student at BCW.

David Davies arrived on the mission field in November 1937 and began to learn Swahli, "A very hard language" he said which had been introduced by King Wana, before that there was many tribal languages and it was all "mixed up." David eventually served in the Congo for twenty-seven years.

It was on the mission field that he met his wife Anne, who had studied at a Holiness Bible College in the UK, she had arrived in the Congo in 1943. They married in March 1949 whilst on furlough in Blackheath, Birmingham, England. Anne told me how David had said to her that he would look after her, she responded with a chuckle in her voice, "I made it to the mission field on my own!"

David informed me how he and his fellow labourers, some of whom were pastors built a church, brick by brick which "took a long time." On the wall of his home he pointed out the large colour photo of the church which appeared to be approximately one hundred feet long by forty feet wide where revival first broke out on his mission station at Wamba. Alongside this photo was an A4 sized facial shot of an aged native who had been saved under C. T. Studd's ministry who began his work in the Congo in 1913. There was also one other picture of a native in traditional costume on his knees in a posture of prayer.

David said, "There was lots of prayer before the revival came" and when it came "it was frightening to behold with all the people falling on the ground." His wife Anne told me that, "There was one young lady who did not go to bed until 2am for weeks" because she was praying for God to move.

In July 1953, they travelled seventy miles to Lubutu, the head mission station, where revival first broke out in February 1953 and returned to their large mission station at Wamba with a native evangelist, Tomu and his wife. Lumbtu had witnessed a visitation of the Spirit in 1950, which was documented in *A Mighty Work of the Spirit* by Norman Grubb (c.1950).

The Wamba station had been founded in 1931 by the William's and soon grew into the largest WEC mission station in the Congo with between four and five hundred people living on site, including three hundred children. Daisy Kingdom was in charge of the boys and Anne Thomas in charge of the girls, "We were head cooks and bottle washers" said Anne Davies whose main role was to look after the pre-schoolers.

In October 1953, David and Anne wrote an account of the revival at their mission station under the chapter 'Overwhelming Floods' which can be found in the book *This is That* originally published by the CLC in 1954; his brother's story is told under the chapter 'Tornado of Blessing.'

On Thursday the 16 July 1953; Prayer Day, the evangelist Tomu spoke from Exodus 19:11 'Let them be ready for the third day. For on the third day the Lord will come...' Anne said, "We were quite expecting something to happen, but were disappointed." Three days later on the Sunday, God came and revival continued in and around their mission compound for the next three to four years. Anne was not present on that Sunday morning as she had to attend to a baby and stated that David was used more during the revival than she was "because of the little ones."

At the end of the Sunday service, as the congregation were leaving, a paralysed girl call Biboko began to wail and cry out under conviction of sin which became louder and louder, the congregation returned to the church, the revival had begun and the conviction spread.

Back at the bungalow, where Anne was, a crowd had gathered and there was a lot of crying and repentance, "School girls particularly" said Anne, "The Holy Spirit brought conviction on many of them," after time "it was a changed place, quite a bit of restitution" and soon the kindergarten was taken over from Anne by about half a dozen African helpers because of their zeal to help, so she could focus more on the prep-school with its "120-130 little angels."

Anne told me that there were a dozen or more Greek shopkeepers, merchants whose shops were either side of a dirt road, "there were dirt roads everywhere, red earth, if you dropped anything on it, it would be discoloured immediately" she said. The main shopkeeper was called Constiou and he also had tools returned to him and many of the shopkeepers received restitution from the school children in the form of returned francs.

When asked whether any of the merchants were saved during the revival, Anne could not remember but stated that it must have made a big impression on them. When asked about other accounts of restitutions, Anne informed me that her "headwoman confessed to stealing eggs from under the fowl" and so tried to repay them. Anne said, "A good many used to fall on the ground" under conviction of sin, rolling around, not something that you would willingly want to do, especially amongst the red staining dirt. Though Anne, referring to the schoolgirls, said, "You knew when it was worked up or real – they used to be good imitators – I banged their heads together!"

The revival spread from the WEC mission stations and touched the Pentecostals. Anne told me that because of the revival their station was "a new station." When I asked about the statistics of conversion whether it ran into hundreds or thousands, Anne responded that it was "hundreds in the immediate area," and "not thousands" so confirmed David. The revival "lasted from three to four years" said Anne, "the mission asked us to come home on furlough, we should have refused, it's not something you see everyday." They arrived home in October 1957, the revival was still going and thus the Congo Revival lasted four years, though undoubtedly the afterglow continued.

In the college meeting (a decade ago), the Rev. David Davies gave the reason why it would now appear that a revival never even took place in the Congo. He read from the book of Judges, "When all that generation had been gathered to their fathers, another generation arose after them who did not know the Lord nor the work which He had done for Israel" (Judges 2:10). Revival sometimes precedes a time of judgment or persecution, which prepares the Church for the hardships to come. In the mid 1960s, independence, followed by civil war tore the Belgian Congo apart under the Simba Rising. *This is No Accident* by Leonard C. J. Moules (1965) gives testimonies of the trials encountered by WEC missionaries whilst the *Congo Saga* by David W. Truby (1965) focuses on those connected with the Unevangelized Fields Mission.

After a little more than an hour, I felt it was time for me to leave and asked the retired missionaries if they would pray for me. Anne prayed, and what a prayer, I only wished I had a Digital Voice Recorder instead of my notepad and pen. In part of the prayer she thanked the Lord for the Congo Revival and what they had witnessed, "Lord we want to see it in our homeland...Many more lives transformed...We badly need it...We need revival in Britain."[17] Amen to that.

North Uist Revival (1957-1958)

The Outer Hebrides, Scotland, UK, were first described by the Greek historian Diodus Silculus in 55BC, then by Pliny the Elder (a Roman writer from the first century and not to be confused with Pliney the Younger, the governor of Bithynia from 111-113AD) and also by Ptolemy (an Egyptian astronomer from the second century). The Outer Hebrides extend in a north-easterly direction from Berneray in the south (not to be confused with Bernera in the north) for about 113 miles to the Butt of Lewis. The Outer Hebrides are divided from the Inner Hebrides and from the north-western coast of Scotland by the Hebridean Sea, the Little Minch and the Great Minch.

The islands of North Uist, Benbecula and South Uist, including their causeways are just forty-one miles long and were popularly known as the Long Island from the eighteenth century to the *mid twentieth century (though prior to that the entire Outer Hebrides were known as the Long Island), though, *the causeways at that time were not yet built. The islands were formed from fundamental rock – gneiss, traversed by grains of granite and trap. The soil is peat bog (a good source of fuel for the fire when dried) and varies in depth from a few inches to twenty-feet.[1]

One traveller to the Western Isles during the summer and autumn of 1938, in reference to the Long Island, in his book, *Hebridean Journey* wrote: 'Only in three places are trees to be seen, and in South Uist I cannot recall even one.' One twenty-first century travel guide states that 'the Outer Hebrides are bleak, remote and treeless. The climate is fierce – the islands are completely exposed to the gales that sweep in from the Atlantic, and it rains for more than 250 days of the year.' Though when I visited in April 2005, I saw three sheltered pine trees which were no taller than myself and there was rain showers nearly every day.

The Gaelic Bible translation (for the Gaelic speakers of the Islands and Highlands of Scotland) was completed by 1801 and in 1811 the Gaelic Schools Society (GSS) was founded with its primarily aim to teach Gaelic exclusively. Its agents were to work in one locality for three years and then move on. By 1825, the GSS had seventy-seven schools with 4,300 pupils. John Ferguson who was converted in the North Uist Revival (1957-1958) went into full-time Christian ministry and later documented the revival. He wrote: 'One of the contributing factors to the revivals in the Highlands and Islands in the nineteenth century was the publishing of the Gaelic Bible and the excellent work of the Gaelic Schools Society.' The fiftieth Annual Report (1861) of the GSS also linked its work with the numerous revivals in many districts.

North Uist first saw revival in 1820 under the itinerant preacher, Finlay Munro; in 1844 under Rev. Norman MacLeod; in 1846 at a Gaelic School and in 1880 under lay evangelist Donald Stewart.[2]

The Island of North Uist is only seventeen miles long by twelve miles wide and was not touched during the Lewis Revival (1949-1952) under Rev. Duncan Campbell. The North Uist Revival (1957-1958), 'according to the testimony of some local ministers…was in some respects even greater than the previous movement in Lewis. The movement began and was carried on in at atmosphere of believing prayer and through the faithful preaching of the instruments whom God chose.'[3]

In April 1957, four 'pretty girl evangelists' in their twenties (as a newspaper reporter referred to them) from the Faith Mission (Edinburgh) arrived on North Uist and 'rocked the island.' They were: Mary Morrison (now Mary Peckham), Jean Wilson (now Blanshard), Daphne Parker and Margaret MacIntyre. They held meetings in Carinish in the hamlet of Clachan and did door to door work, whilst wearing the Faith Mission's traditional black straw bonnets. After two weeks they moved to nearby Locheport. Mary Morrison's testimony of her conversion during the Lewis Revival (1949-1952) is in the booklet *Hearken O Daughter! – Mary Morrison* (1966) and with her husband, Colin Peckham, they wrote *Sounds From Heaven – The Revival on the Isle of Lewis 1949-1952* (2004).

Workers from the Faith Mission are traditionally referred to as Pilgrims. In October 1957, the four Pilgrims returned to Claddach Carinish, North Uist, for three weeks, but their mission in North Uist lasted a combined total of eight months! They ministered in the principle towns and villages of Lochmaddy (beginning on the 19 November 1957), Solas (beginning on the 19 January 1958), Tigharry (beginning on the 23 February) and Bayhead beginning in early April until late May 1958 and included in their ministry some smaller villages. Before leaving, Mary Morrison spoke at meetings across the island and held meetings on the smaller islands of Eigg, Rum and Muck (Inner Hebrides). Jean Wilson and Mary Morrison returned in late November 1958 to see how the new converts were doing, held meetings across the island and in December held a mission in Carnish.

The four Pilgrim workers travelled across the island holding evangelistic campaigns in the various villages for several weeks, to a month at a time as the Spirit led. Sometimes they would work in pairs and at other times all four of them would be working together. Generally, the meetings were about two hours long, in both English and Gaelic and a prayer meeting was held afterwards in which seekers could call upon God in prayer and join with the believers. As people were drawn to Christ other ministers were called upon to assist in the work, including the Rev. Duncan Campbell (who frequented the island for several days or weeks at a time), a couple of local ministers, and Joshua Daniel from Madras, India of the Laymen's Evangelical Fellowship.

'The Highlands of Scotland have always been slow to recognise the ministry of women,' so wrote the Rev. Duncan Campbell and the presbyteries of the Church of Scotland of North Uist had recently voted against the admission of women into eldership. So when the faithful Pilgrims began their ministry in 1957 they endured their share of opposition and 'the islanders were somewhat suspicious of women preachers' so wrote John Ferguson.

In Lochmaddy, the ministers had told the people not to assist the women in lodgings; so they booked themselves into a poor house even though at this time, seven other districts were pleading for their help, but they knew that this was where God had called them too.

Mary Morrison recalled: 'When we arrived in Lochmaddy, the people had never before seen Pilgrims of the Faith Mission. First of all, when they saw us with our queer bonnets, they though we were nuns, and of course, they looked upon on very, very suspiciously.'[4]

For two weeks the Pilgrims prayed and pleaded with God's promise to, 'pour water on the dry ground' (Isaiah 43:3) until they knew revival would come. Within a short space of time two homes were opened to the Pilgrims, so two of them went into each home. The team had brought a portable organ with them and they began to sing hymns in the village hall meetings (the ministers refused them the use of the churches), 'but the locals were so interested in the organ that they wouldn't sing the hymns.' The organ was sent back to the mainland and so they 'sang without the organ and the people began to learn the hymns.'

'The spiritual atmosphere deepened night after night, and the devil lifted his head, his ugly head. Some people in the village began to say all manner of things about us', which were lewd, crude and rude. 'The clerk of the county began to spread around rumours that we would make the people mental if they believed what we were saying. The people began to listen to the stories but still came to the meetings.'[5]

After two weeks, with the assurance of revival, they called for Rev. Duncan Campbell to assist them, organised a meeting and around forty people attended as they had heard that a minister was coming. They began preaching inside the poor house to those assembled, inside the old rickety hall. The Rev. Duncan Campbell was still suffering from the effects of a fourteen-hour seasick crossing, due to an intense storm that had greatly delayed the ferry. Rev. Duncan Campbell later said, "I had never been in such a meeting!" as one of the Pilgrims spoke on the rich man and Lazarus for an hour often quoting John Bunyan, "Listen to the sighs from hell!" and from that moment the North Uist Revival broke out as someone let out a cry and people began to tremble.[6] The speaker asked Rev. Campbell to end the meeting and they left the work to God. At midnight over thirty people came to their lodgings seeking the Saviour! The next morning the church was crowded and the minister could not understand because no one had arranged a meeting, but the fear of God swept the community.

Mary Morrison noted the start of the revival: 'Then one night the break came. After weeks of preaching we made an appeal. The first night, when we saw the people getting up here and there, seeking Christ, we were nearly bowled over. My, we hardly expected that! Souls began to come to Christ. The Spirit of God began to be outpoured. The local barman was saved [the barman at the hotel]. Then instead of the bar being crowded, packed to capacity on Saturday nights, one Saturday there were only seven men lounging about. The manager of the hotel began to get a little worried because he wasn't get rid of his whisky!"[7]

In December 1957, Margaret MacIntyre and Jean Wilson returned to the mainland to attend conferences. They were involved in a car accident due to ice on the roads and were unable to return to North Uist until the third week of January 1958. Mary Morrison and Daphne Parker held a Watch Night service for the new converts so that they could see in the New Year of 1958 in a spirit of praise and worship instead of the former drunkenness and dancing. It was reported that the New Years bar takings at the Lochmaddy hotel 'were dramatically reduced!' One publican told a newspaper reporter that his sales were down by £100 per day over the Festive Season of Christmas and New Year.[8]

In mid January 1958, after six weeks of ministry in Lochmaddy, the Pilgrims went to the school in the parish of Solas (which consists of four very small villages linked via a single track road, as is much of the island) and asked the headmaster if they could use the stone-built building to hold evening services. He replied, "You'll get no joy here" but nonetheless consented to their request. At the evening service, many people gave their lives to the Lord and even the headmaster inquired about his own soul.

I visited the island of North Uist in 2005 whilst on a mission. The small stone-built school is still there today on the edge of Middle Quarter, Solas. Like many of the communities in the Hebrides, you cannot truly appreciate how isolated some of the communities and houses are unless you visit such a place. In the twenty-first century, car ownership is generally the norm, but fifty or sixty years ago most people had to catch the bus, cycle or travel on foot and the elements in the Hebrides are unmerciful and the wind is piercing. Try to visualise the natural elements and landscape in the context of people being drawn to church or attending religious meetings, often in the bleakest of weather conditions, especially in winter snows. Only nineteen people in the Solas area did not attend the meetings and most of them were aged and infirm and therefore unable to come. Whilst I am not sure of the exact population at the time, based on the number of houses I saw in 2005 (and the size of the small stone-built school), a population of less than one hundred in 1957 would not be far wrong. So we could say that approximately eighty percent of the village attended the meetings. For some nights the school hall was packed and even the side-rooms were used for overflow!

John Ferguson wrote: 'The secondary school children travelled daily in the bus to Bayhead School [approximately twenty miles away] and all the way they sang the hymns and Gospel songs [from the meetings]. The whole place was aware that an unusual visitation from the Lord was taking place. One day the children themselves turned the dancing class at school into a meeting where they all sang the hymns which they had learned.

'On a few occasions, some of the children arranged the seats as in a meeting and conducted their own! No-one was allowed in when they held their meetings and the cleaners at times listened at the key-hole as one sang, another prayed, another read and as they continued to seek the Lord in their prayers and activities.'

At Tigharry, a rural area, meetings began in February 1958 and 111 people attended the first night, many coming from Solas and snow was on the ground. Mary Morrison noted: 'The teenagers came through the snow with their bicycles...but nobody seemed to feel either the cold or the wind.' There were so many children at the meetings that 'at times' so noted John Ferguson, 'the room would be so crowded that they would be perched on the windowsills or wherever they could find a place.' Special meetings were arranged for the children and 'many young lives were touched by the Spirit of God.' Miss Daphne Parker took the children meetings and often used visual aids, such as flannelgraphs to illustrate Bible stories and to help the children understand better, the simple truths of salvation, which allowed the little children to come to Jesus (Mark 10:14).

Kate-Ann Shirran, a child of eleven who was converted during one of the children's meetings recalled, "I remember well that the talk in the playground at the interval time centred on those who had been saved the night before. Hymn-singing was also part of the playtime at school."[9]

At Tigharry the four Pilgrim "spinsters" as Mary Morrison referred to her team, stayed at the house of a 'very respectable' unconverted (though God-fearing) bachelor who had a large house. He said, "Now don't ask me for anything! Just open the drawers and find things for yourself...All I want is for you to make my meals when I come in from the farm. That's all I want." He was converted at one of the meetings.[10]

The small team of Pilgrims travelled around the island of North Uist from door to door, holding meetings in various locations and the Holy Spirit gave blessing to their labours over the next several months. The Rev. Duncan Campbell, speaking a few years after the revival quoted from the local press, "The drink trade in North Uist has been ruined!" One of the pilgrims in a letter wrote: 'Three prayer meetings are held every week in every parish!' The team of four left in May 1958.[11]

Indonesian Revival (1964-1974)

Indonesia has over 13,000 islands, 3,000 of which are inhabited and including its seas is the same size as America. Geographically the Indonesian Archipelago is shaped like a curved banana, 3,000 miles long and from north to south 1,500 miles, though the actual land mass is a lot thinner.

To date, in its breadth of miracles, the Indonesian Revival is the most supernatural revival the world has ever seen (and was very controversial in its day) with signs and wonders that boggle the mind. During the revival, literally hundreds of disciples of the Lord Jesus Christ, participated in and saw signs and wonders of truly biblical proportions, however, it was not always like this.

The vast majority of miracles took place on the island of Timor on the eastern extremity of the Indonesian archipelago. For this reason this revival though not confined to Timor is sometimes referred to as the Timor Revival (1965-1974). It started a year later than in other places of Indonesia and continued for three years longer, though the afterglow in many places was still strong after these dates.

In 1964, a revival broke out on the Island of Rote (also known as Roti), fifteen miles south of Timor as the word of the Lord was preached. Two men, Pak Elias and Pastor Gideon (who first met in 1966) were both figures at the forefront and natives of Rote. Prayer groups sprang up which became the backbone of the revival. As they preached the saving message of the cross, the locals became overwhelmed in their sins and called on the Saviour and within a year a thousand people had been converted. When Kurt Koch visited in 1969, the news reached him that thirty temples had been burnt to the ground by former heathen worshippers. Now Christians, they also burned all their fetishes and charms.[1]

On the island of Sumatra (a thousand miles away) God began a work amongst the Muslim 'poison mixers' on the southern tip when their tribal leader, Abram decided to tell his people about the story of Bethlehem. He had just finished attending a Communist educational course when he heard the Good News through an open window of a church whilst a Christmas sermon was in progress. Abram sent a letter to some Christians asking for help as his people wanted to hear more about the Christ-child. The help duly arrived and within five years, 1,500 were converted.[2]

I spoke to someone who was ministering on the Island of Sumatra in late 2000 as part of a mission team. He told me that the island has large numbers of believers and the local pastors that he met still speak of revival with warm affection and some said that they were still in the midst of revival.

From October to December 1964, a Healing Campaign was held on the island of Timor under Johannes Ratuwalu where several thousand people were healed, but sadly the message of repentance was not prominent and according to local reports, Ratuwalu 'succumbed to the excess of his pride' which brought the movement to a premature end.[3]

450,000 inhabitants out of more than one million belonged to the former Dutch Reformed Church, but there were only 103 pastors, so the church, though statistically strong was not healthy due to lack of pastors. From 1963-1968 church communion attendance in Indonesia went up twenty-fold. Within one year of the revival, 80,000 people were converted, (half were former Communists and half were former heathen), 15,000 had been healed and over 100,000 fetishes had been publicly destroyed, often by fire. Some churches which had about 30 Christians rocketed to 500 in the same space of time. While on one island, virtually all of its 20,000 inhabitants became Christians, where prior to the revival there were less than one hundred Christians![4]

From January to February 1965, Benjamin Manuain began two months of evangelistic meetings 'to supply what had been lacking in the Healing Campaign,' (repentance and Christ-centred preaching) and according to Rev. J. M.E. Daniel of Soe, this marked the beginning of the revival.[5]

In July 1965, David Simeon arrived on Timor with an evangelistic team from the Bible School in East Java, (Indonesian Bible Institute in Batu) including the rector, Detmar Scheunemann; they stayed for two months. The message was of repentance, rebirth and sanctification, and this became known as the official birthday of the revival according to Kurt Koch. The Christians got cleaned up and on fire for God and the natives piled their fetishes high and publicly burned them.[6]

At the time of the revival, the island of Timor had few roads and was mostly jungle with tracks traversing the difficult terrain. Up until 1971 (and at least till 1974 during the rainy season), the only public transportation between Kupang on the coast and Soe, seventy miles inland was a Timorese truck. A typical Timorese home was a circular hut with grass roof and dirt floor.[7]

Melchior Tari, (known as Mel amongst his friends) was a youthful man in his twenties who lived in the village of Soe. He belonged to the traditional Dutch Presbyterian Church, where everything was written down, including the sermons and the prayers. They were taught in all sincerity that healings, miracles and the gifts of the Holy Spirit were from a bygone age, the age of the Jesus' twelve disciples, yet the Christians thought nothing of going to see the witchdoctor for healing!

In Soe, on the 26 September 1965, about two hundred people of all ages were inside the Dutch Presbyterian Church. As they were praying, a sound from heaven like a mighty rushing wind swept through the church. The people began to pray in unison, which was not done in Mel's church, even Mel thought, 'They have forgotten the written order!' The two pastors at the front of the church were a little perplexed not knowing what to do. Opposite the church was a police station, one of the officers on duty saw flames rising from the roof of the church. He rang the fire bell to inform the villagers to come quickly as the entire village was expected to help out, not having any fire engines. As they approached, they saw the flames, but no damage. More than 800 additional people filled the church that night, making more than 1,000. Many came under conviction of sin and were converted and baptised in the Holy Spirit alongside the traditional Presbyterians. People began to raise their hands and worship the Lord and some spoke in a tongue which was unknown to them and which they had never learnt (including English, French, German and Hebrew). Some of these worshipers were illiterate including one woman who only spoke her tribal language of Timorese, 'who began to pray out loud in very beautiful perfect English.' Mel wrote: 'Heaven came down that night and it was wonderful.'

People began to stand on their feet. Those who had given their lives to the Lord, 'ran to their houses and got their witchcraft materials,' fetishes, astrology stuff, dirty books and 'their books on how to interpret dreams and they brought them back to the church and burned them all in a fire.' People confessed their sins and the service went on until midnight. Before the end of the service a laymen stood up and read out Acts 2:17, 'It shall comes to pass in the last days...' He then preached for thirty minutes and told the people that the Lord had revealed to him that it was the Church's responsibility (the laypeople) to go and preach the Good News. This is the duty of every Christian and it had to begin tomorrow.[8]

The first missionary teams were formed in September 1965, under Pastor Joseph, the superintendent of the Presbytery in Soe. Within three months there were seventy teams and they preached the word with signs following. Within three years, 200,000 had been converted.

On the 1 October 1965, the Communists tried to take over the country, but failed, this led to a bloody backlash by the Indonesian Muslims. In later years some of the converts became missionaries in other lands. Eight of the evangelistic teams from Soe, consisted of children aged from six to ten and their ministry was just as powerful as the adults. They moved in the gifts of the Holy Spirit, participated in intercession and saw conversions and healings as they trekked up to fifteen miles through the jungle to other villages.

The adult evangelistic teams lived by faith and were guided by the Holy Spirit, and saw supernatural events and results. Drunks got sober, natives destroyed their fetishes, and some tore down their temples; Muslims saw Jesus as the Son of God, wrongs were righted and many illiterate people (especially women) received visions and were called to go and preach under the leading of the Holy Spirit. Sermons of five hours were common and could be as long as fifteen hours as the people were hungry for the word of the Lord, and the sense of time was lost in the presence of God. Crowds flocked to hear these preachers.

Father Dennis Bennett, an Episcopalian Priest (American Anglican), who can be accredited as the father of the Charismatic Renewal which began in his church in 1960, had a missionary friend who was the head of a strong interdenominational missionary fellowship. He returned from Indonesia in the late 1960s and said, "I tramped seventy miles into the interior [probably Soe] – it was seventy miles to get a glimpse of heaven as I heard these ex-Communists and ex-Mohammedans singing all day long the praise of the true God for the joy He has brought them.

"I was a missionary in Indonesia many years ago. We would work for a year to get one convert from Mohammedanism to Christ, and then half the time he would recant. Now the Christians who used to be Mohammedans are organising evangelistic teams to go to Pakistan to win other Mohammedans to Christ! It is incredible!"[9]

In Mel Tari's church, God dealt with the people's sin in a very personal way. Often someone would have a word of knowledge and confront the person concerned. If they denied their sin, e.g. adultery the person with the word of knowledge would state the details, name, places, dates etc.! The sin of owning alcohol was very prevalent on the island of Timor (as well as smoking) and this sin was confessed and put away. One Christian was told that he had alcohol hidden in his home, he denied it. He was told, "If you do not repent within twenty-four hours you will die." He still denied it and didn't care about the warning, being in sin and unbelief. He came to church the next day and was told that he had one hour to repent. With five minutes to go, the Church urged him to repent, he still denied his secret sin. The minutes passed, the Church begged him to repent, thirty second remained and he thought the people were crazy. Some began to count down the seconds, 9, 8, 7...1. The man fell down dead. Mel, writing in 1971, stated that God so changed his village of Soe in Timor that if you could find just one glass of alcohol, he would be really surprised.[10]

Prior to the revival, alcohol had been used in the communion service. But after people had repented of their sins they refused to partake of communion because of the alcohol. There were no grapes in Timor so the pastor and his flock began to use tea with sugar. After some time they felt that they should use the same thing that Jesus and the apostles used. Since October 1967, they would draw water from the well, pray over it (often for an hour) and the Lord turned it into purple non-alcoholic wine. More than sixty times this miracle was performed in Mel's church![11]

During the revival under the Indonesian 'umbrella' multitudes were converted, nominal Christians, Muslims and the animists or heathen, (including pagan priests and their followers). The enemy had ruled for far too long and like a flood, the Spirit of the Lord raised a standard against him. Thousands were set free from demonic oppression, delivered from demons and curses and sorcery were defeated. Also, all the gifts of the Holy Spirit were restored to the once traditional churches of Indonesia, though not every church and its pastor approved of such things.

One team arrived at a certain village and began to preach. The pagan priest told them that they had served the devil for generations and that he had done them well, giving them healings and rain when they asked. The pagan priest threw down a challenge, (just like Elijah on Mount Carmel), 'let Him prove that He is more powerful.' The team did not know what to do and began to ask the Lord for direction. He revealed to them that they must gather the followers of the pagan priest together and let them see for themselves the power of God. About 1,000 assembled, with the priest out in front and the team opposite them. The team lifted their hands to heaven and prayed, glorifying the Lord. They bound the demons in the name of Jesus, mentioned the precious blood shed at Calvary and commanded the demonic powers to depart in the name of Jesus. Soon the pagan priest began to tremble, cry and he surrendered his life to Jesus! The team were a little perplexed to see such instant results, perhaps they were waiting for the fire to descend as in Elijah's day. The priest knew many of the demons by name, but after the demonic powers had been bound, he saw them with his eyes and heard them with his ears, gather together as one. They ran away crying out, 'Jesus won't permit us to stay here. We must go because Jesus wants these people.' The entire tribe gave their lives to the Lord![12]

During the revival the signs and wonders were outstanding, the blind saw, the deaf heard, the lame walked, the lepers were healed, the dead were raised (about ten to fifteen cases, even after two days and in the tropical heat bodies begin to decompose after six hours), the waters were calmed, the rain was commanded to stop; all in the name of Jesus. People received visions and dreams, words of knowledge, prophecy and extraordinary discernment – knowing the secrets of men's hearts; whilst others received songs from God, a few were taught by angels (being illiterate) and Jesus even appeared Himself to others.

Mel Tari wrote: 'One of the characteristics of the Indonesian Revival is that before we go out and preach, the Lord gives us all the details of what we should do. We write it down on paper and then follow it exactly as it is. If He tells us to stop at this place or minister in that place, we do just what the Lord tells us.'[13]

Some of the missionary teams ate supernatural food (manna from heaven), they were protected from crocodiles as they waded or swam across rivers, one team walked across the Noemina River, the largest in Timor at 300 yards wide and from 20-30 feet deep during the flood season. The water did not come above their knees and they felt their feet on the riverbed! Some of the pagans and Christians (who were not part of the team) after witnessing this event, stepped in the river and nearly drowned. One team often saw flames of fire over the churches where they preached at, others saw supernatural light, which guided their footsteps by night, one mission team was transported in the Spirit, others witnessed food multiplying, and food not going-over in the tropical heat. In one place the house shook as they prayed as in Acts 4 and a church (not Mel's) saw water turning into communion wine (non-alcoholic) which was the tastiest ever; this happened on at least ten occasions! Other teams were protected from the elements, clouds by day in the intense tropical heat; others were protected from the rain as they trekked to other villages while it was raining ten feet in front of them, behind them and to each side of them!

The Bible School in East Java played a significant role in the revival as converts were trained and then went forth with the Good News in the power of the Spirit. In 1967, the wind of the Spirit swept through the School bringing deep repentance and reconciliation between staff and students who had previously been at odds with each other.

During an eighteen-day missionary campaign in West Irian (modern day West Papua) nearly 3,000 people were converted. 250 young men dedicated themselves to full-time Gospel work and an offering of £400 was collected (a colossal amount for poor Indonesians / Papua New Guineans, especially in the late 1960s) and included items of jewellery. The evangelising and revival did not go without its opposition and persecution. God's judgment was poured out on many a person who stood in His way, some died whilst others were afflicted by the hand of God, but there was also at least one Christian martyr.[14]

In 1970, God called Mel to America with the message: 'You need to get back to the simplicity of the word of God, not only back to the Bible, but back to the simplicity of the word.' Mel has since preached on all six continents, married Nona Rea (an American) and is known as the eyewitness chronicler of the Indonesian Revival.[15]

Evangelist, Roy Hession first visited Indonesia (the island of Java) in 1963 with William Nagenda, a revivalist who had been used in the East Africa Revival (1930s-1950s) and especially in Uganda. Roy returned in 1972 with a small team and revisited the Batu Bible School, Java. He noted that on Timor, that there was hardly a miracle in the New Testament that had not been reproduced on that island, but sadly for many young converts their focus was more on the miracles than the Lord Himself. If they did not see the miracles, 'they forced them, or rather simulated them. This had caused much scandal among the church leaders, not all of whom were in sympathy with the revival, that they vowed that they would not have any more preachers from Batu.' Roy and his team were to travel to Timor, but their visit had to be cancelled for this reason. After Roy had returned home to England he heard that 'the trouble on Timor had been resolved.'[16]

The above incident must have been resolved in a matter of months and was not mentioned by Mel Tari, though the lessons of it were recorded by his wife whom he married in May 1972, whilst in America. Nona Tari wrote about the difference in culture and the things that she observed when she first arrived on Timor in September 1972. She wrote: 'Indonesian Christians do *not* talk about miracles – except to the person they consider their spiritual advisors...[They] also have a fear of robbing God of some of His glory by setting the persons He used on a pedestal...There is always a danger that Christians will take their eyes off the Lord and instead fasten them on what He does...The Timorese Christians have sidestepped this danger by keeping the Lord Jesus and His love uppermost in their minds and by assigning miracles to their proper place in the background.'[17]

Kurt Koch in a written rebuttal (a four page pamphlet), noted that Petrus Octavianus, was 'the most powerful spiritual leader in the revival' and that 'between the years 1963-1969' he (Kurt) 'was in Indonesia five times including the great miracle period at the beginning of the revival.' He wrote: 'I do not have a mania for miracles... yet there are miracles which I consistently affirm, the miracle that God's Son is Saviour, the miracle of the filling with the Holy Spirit...The history of revivals shows us that at the beginning of many revivals miracles have appeared. This occurred in Wales in 1905, in Korea in 1906-1960, in Uganda in 1927, in Ethiopia among the Wallamo 1937-1948, in Timor in 1965-1969, as well as in other places. I have travelled throughout the world. I have always asked the Lord for the ability to discern that which is genuine from that which is false.

'The miracles are not the essential things. To be sure, every mania for miracles is dangerous. Yet it has pleased God to bring about many miracles at the outpouring of the Holy Spirit. All revivals are characterised by similar phenomena. Moreover the miracles in Indonesia have decreased in number since the illiterate people have learned to read the Bible. This is a healthy development.'[18]

Argentinean Revival (1982-1997)

In June 1951 there was a revival at City Bell Bible College, just outside of Buenos Aires, Argentina, which had been recently founded by American missionary, Dr. Edward Miller. This revival and the intercession that followed prepared Buenos Aires for the unknown American healing evangelist, Tommy Hicks. He first felt called of God to hold a campaign in Argentina in late 1951 and arrived in April 1954. For sixty days he held a campaign in Buenos Aires, with President Peron's full approval which saw a total attendance of up to six million visitors and around 20,000 converts (18,000 joined local churches) which, at the time was the biggest ingathering in Argentina's history.[1]

Dr. Edward Miller arrived in Argentina in the late 1940s and witnessed 'seven great revivals' in his 'prolific ministry' so recorded Lila Turhune in *Cross Pollination* (1999). During the Brownsville Revival (1995-2000) she was the head intercessor.

In the preface to Edward Miller's book, *The Flaming Flame* (1973), the question was asked, "What has been happening since the time of the Hick's revival in Argentina?" Miller responded: '*The Flaming Flame* is my answer...it is the sharing of the continued and glorious working of Divine grace and mercy copiously poured out upon this land – the southernmost land of the world, from 1954 to 1968. Is it by accident or by Divine design that the southernmost part of Argentina is called Tierra del Fuego or "Land of the Fire?" '

Ed Silvoso, Director of Harvest Evangelism in an interview with Noel Stanton, senior pastor of the Jesus Fellowship, was talking about the 1954 Revival under Tommy Hicks. Ed Silvoso said, "There was another revival in the mid-60s with Juan Carlos Ortiz, who wrote the book *Disciple*. But they made a mistake at the very beginning. They said this revival is for the Church not for the lost, and it became self-centred and led to many divisions. There were blessings, but never the breakthrough."[2]

In Argentina, the years 1976 to 1983 were years of oppressive dictatorship under evil military rule. The "Dirty War" in which people were detained in the middle of the night by the army or police for no apparent reason had claimed up to 80,000 lives. The Roman Catholic Church had sway over the mass of people and many Argentineans had intertwined Christianity and native occult practice which were rampant across the country. Daily, witches, warlocks and other occult members appeared on national television to talk about their practices. The economy was a disaster; inflation was over one thousand percent! The loss of the Falkland War of 1982, over the Malvinas Islands between Argentina and Britain, shocked the proud nation who had been told by the military propaganda machine that they were winning. All these events were instrumental in breaking the spirit of the Argentineans so that they would long for truth – and as Jesus declared, "I am the Way the Truth and the Life."

Prior to the revival which began in 1982 (which for the first few years was largely confined to Buenos Aires) there was a team of intercessors in a village in Zimbabwe, Africa, led by Rhodesian born, Michael Howard (who is no stranger to revival). They had been led by the Holy Spirit to pray that a war would arise between Argentina and Britain. The Holy Spirit said, "My work in that land [Argentina] was never completed and now is the hour." Michael Howard wrote: 'I came to realise after a while that it was not so much that the Lord wanted Britain to win that war, but He wanted Argentina to lose. One of the intercessors, a lady, had a picture of a man seated on a throne, wearing three crowns. He was looking south and was very much involved in Argentina.

The intercessions prior to the City Bell Bible College Revival (1951) had broken one of the three powers that enslaved the nation – the spiritualist Eva Peron (the Argentine Presidents wife). More than two decades later, unaware of Dr. Edwards Miller's ministry and the 1951 revival (which they only found out years later), the Spirit revealed to the African team that the tentacles of Rome and the military also had to be broken.

The Holy Spirit spoke, "I want the defeat of Argentina because when she is defeated the military Junta will be overthrown ending dictatorship forever in that land. And, with the overthrow of the Junta, the power of Rome will also be forever broken. No force will be able to prevent Me from freely presenting the Gospel in Argentina again."

The African team began to intercede but the heavens were like brass. A twenty-one day fast was called. They were given to prayer every night and throughout the day as people could come. Many of the intercessors began to do some research about the country, its history and geography to see if anything prevailed. Michael Howard wrote: 'The burden was heavy as we began to carry Argentina like a baby, travailing and crying out to the Lord to birth a mighty deliverance for her tens of millions.'

It was after the fast that the breakthrough came through the book of Ezekiel, when the Lord put His hooks into the jaws of Gog to bring them against Israel (Ezekiel 38:3-12). They prayed 'for the Lord to put His hooks into Argentina and draw her against Britain.' They 'saw in the Spirit a huge bushfire raging up the entire continent beginning from Argentina and devouring everything in its wake that was not from God.' Whole nights were spent praising the Lord when they knew victory was assured, soon, 'Argentina was forgotten' as the team interceded for other nations, until the following month when they heard that war had been declared.[3]

President Galtieri ordered the invasion of the island. The war cost the lives of 255 British personnel, three islanders and 655 Argentineans. Argentinean, Claudio Freidzon wrote: 'It was the sorrow and suffering of our nation that prepared hearts for the Gospel. The Malvinas (Falkland Islands) war left a tremendous wound in people's hearts. We lived through days of tension and deep sadness as a consequence of the death of many innocent boys in that frigid place. Our pride was shattered by defeat. In the spiritual arena, this situation led to the willingness of many people to open up to the Lord.'[4]

Carlos Annacondia, a successful and wealthy nut and bolts businessman was converted in 1979. When he had fully consecrated his life to Christ, he felt the call of an evangelist. Within less than two years his evangelistic campaigns under his ministry, Message of Salvation began. It included lively worship, a simple Gospel message, deliverance from demons, prayer for healing and prayer for the baptism of the Holy Spirit for all believers. He became the key figure of the revival, but others to name just some; Omar Caberera, Pablo Bottarai, Claudio Freidzon, El Silvoso, Luis Palau, Duardo Lorenzo, Juan Zuccarelli, Carlos Mraida and Guillermo Prein also held strategic positions as they worked alongside multiple other lesser known leaders.

In the early days of the Argentinean Revival, it was the lower classes that filled the plots of land (and later the stadiums) under Carlos Annacondia campaigns, which were brightly illuminated, having a carnival atmosphere to draw the crowds in. There were no seats which gave the people freedom to move around so that they did not become restless, food stalls were around the perimeter and a large well-decorated platform was at the front. Behind the platform would be a 150-foot tent with yellow and white stripes, which was known as the 'spiritual intensive care unit' where deliverance took place under the care of numerous counsellors. Trained workers, 'stretcher bearers' as they were deemed would be on the lookout for people manifesting during the preaching (under the influence of demons) and carry them to the tent where they would deliver them in Jesus' name and break the curses and bondages off of people's lives. As time went on, mass deliverance sessions were commenced as the strong man was bound, Jesus' name was invoked and spiritual shackles and chains were broken by the authority that was commissioned to the evangelist on stage.

Carlos Annacondia is a firm believer that beyond basic evangelism, the Great Commission has four aspects based on what Jesus said.

1. Salvation – "Go into all the world and preach the Gospel to every creature" (Mark 16:15).

2. Deliverance from demons – "In My name they will cast out demons" (Mark 16:17).

3. The manifestation of the anointing of the Holy Spirit – "They will speak with new tongues" (Mark 16:17).

4. Healing – "They will lay hands on the sick, and they will recover" (Mark 16:18).[5]

Claudio Freidzon wrote: 'Soon after the military defeat [Falklands War], a tremendous victory was won for the Gospel. We were filled with joy at the sight of five thousand people giving their lives to Jesus Christ [at a campaign held by Carlos Annacondia]. On the following day the same thing happened...'[6]

In an interview with Noel Stanton, Ed Silvoso said the revival started in 1983. He said, "The current move of God began in March 1983, when Carlos Annacondia, less than two years old in the Lord, began to preach with tremendous boldness and led 40,000 people to a public decision. That was so unusual that the church debated whether it was from God or the devil!"[7]

The campaigns progressed from weekend evangelistic meetings to two months with nightly Gospel messages, even under heavy rain and intense cold. As the years progressed, people from other social classes, especially the middle class came to know the Lord in these meetings. Healings were common, signs and wonders were frequent, creative miracles were not unknown; even raising the dead! Deliverance was essential for all new believers along with being filled with the Holy Spirit, discipleship and being committed to a church of whatever denomination or style took the persons preference.

Months before any campaign commenced, prayer (and intercession) would be going up to heaven in which local churches participated and it was these local churches that brought all the volunteers together, including security guards and those who assisted in the deliverance and counselling sessions afterwards.

In some cities, years prior to an evangelistic campaign, spiritual mapping (of an area) would be undertaken, coupled with prayer and intercession. This was to dislodge or disengage a principality; e.g. a territorial stronghold of unbelief over a geographical area. This principality would hinder people from responding to the Gospel, as the god of this age had blinded them. But after prayer and completed intercession(s), the veil of unbelief would be taken away so that they could see the Light and Life of Jesus Christ and call upon Him and be saved.

Ed Silvoso in the introduction to *That None Should Perish – How to Reach Entire Cities for Christ Through Prayer Evangelism* (1994) wrote: 'I will share how God had led me and my ministry team, along with many other pastors in Resistencia, Argentina (population 400,000), to the rediscovery of prayer evangelism...this in turn has resulted in the evangelization of an entire city and the growth of the Church there, far beyond what any other approach has produced before.' *Revival! It Can Transform Your City* (1999) by Peter Wagner and *Storming Hell's Brazen Gates* (1988) by Dick Bernal also covers these aspects of spiritual warfare.

From 1981 to 1985, Carlos Annacondia held twenty-three evangelistic campaigns in the province of Buenos Aires and saw more than 288,000 conversions! But 1984 saw the beginning of great multitudes attending Annacondia's campaigns. In 1984, campaigns were held in La Plata, Ensenda and Tolosa, where 50,000 people came to Christ, the city of Monte Grande saw 8,500 and later that year 83,000 souls were won in Mar del Plata, followed in 1985, by 60,200 converts in San Justo, 57,000 in San Martin and 16,000 in Moreno![8]

In February 1986, Claudio Freidzon, held an evangelistic campaign in the public square of Plaza Noruega in the Belgrano district of Buenos Aires. God moved mightily, one thousand people (Claudio's neighbours) surrendered their lives to Christ in just twenty days, and The King of Kings Church was birthed! There were testimonies of healings, especially those with flatfoot, others whose teeth had been supernaturally filled because they needed fillings.

By December 1992, what had started for Claudio as a personal thirst for more of the Holy Spirit began to impact large crowds. He rented the largest auditorium in Buenos Aires, with 12,000 seats. When the building was full there was still 25,000 people waiting outside! They waited for three hours for the second service. The Assemblies of God, foreign mission magazine, *Mountain Movers*, published an article which stated: '...Though the awakening began in Claudio's church, it extended to hundreds of pastors and churches...'[9]

In 1997, Omar Cabrera, (who began his ministry in the 70s) was known as the 'dean of the revival' and had over 145,000 members in his Vision of the Future [cell] Church. They met in 187 cities across the country; therefore it was a scattered 'centrifugal church' where the senior itinerant pastor (Omar Cabrera) would go to the flock instead of the other way around. Omar Cabrera and his team have also calculated that all those they have reached with the Gospel 'some sixty-four percent have proved to be fruit that remains.'[10]

The Olmos Prison, the largest and highest maximum security prison in Argentina also saw revival when three hundred prisoners came to a 'singing meeting' and were locked in. About one hundred people gave their lives to Jesus. By the end of 1995, out of over 3,200 prisoners, forty-five percent were converted and began holding daily church services. Later the Christians had their own evangelical cell blocks, where formerly the various criminal elements were segregated – but are now one in Christ![11]

After the revival in 1997, (though the afterglow continued for much longer); ten percent of the population of Argentina were evangelical Christians and that's a lot of new churches. There was also the emergence of qualified leadership, greater evangelistic commitment and unity among pastors as they were drawn together as one to hold numerous large campaigns. Old grievances had been repented of between different leaders and denominations. This led to open confession and reconciliation, which is essential to rapid church growth through the blessing of unity (Psalm 133).

The Argentinean Revival, out of the one thousand plus revivals I am aware of, to date, is the fourth longest running revival / awakening in Church History. Lila Turhune wrote: 'The only way true revival reaps a *continual* harvest is for there to be *continual intercession* and obedience to every direction of God.'[12]

Brownsville Revival (1995-2000)

The Brownsville Revival is also known as the Pensacola Revival or the Father's Day Outpouring. The vast majority of the information is a firsthand account of what I saw (and what I heard), when I visited this revival in late July 1997.

In 1992, Dr. David Yonggi Cho from South Korea (who had the largest church in the world) was ministering in Seattle, Washington and began praying for revival in America. As he prayed, he felt the Lord prompt him to get a map of America and to point his finger on the map. It landed on Pensacola, Florida. He sensed the Lord say, "I am going to send revival to the seaside city of Pensacola, and it will spread like fire until all of America has been consumed by it."

For over twenty years, faithful members of the congregation of Brownsville Assembly of God Church in Pensacola, Florida, America, had been praying for revival, but in the last two and a half years prior to the revival breaking out, the Sunday night meeting was given over entirely to prayer, praise and worship.

Pastor John Kilpatrick was fed up with his role at the large, successful church and knew there was more. One night in the early hours, he went into the church, placed his keys on the platform, and cried out to God in desperation for His glory: "God, I want to see You move. If You're not going to send revival here, please send me to a place where You are. I don't care if it's a small congregation in the middle of nowhere with just twenty-five people. Just take me where You're going to move." He walked out and left his keys there. Every Saturday night he returned to pray and the Sunday morning sermon was frequently on the theme of revival.

Evangelist Stephen (Steve) Hill was a former missionary to Argentina during the years 1985-1992 for the Assemblies of God's foreign mission division. He had worked with the Argentine revivalist, Carlos Anacondia who has seen more than one million people come to the Lord during his anointed crusades. Returning to America, Steve Hill, set up Together in the Harvest ministry. On Sunday morning (Father's Day), 18 June 1995, by Pastor Kilpatrick's invite, Steve Hill preached at Brownsville. His text was from Psalm 77, with emphasis on verses 11-12 'I will remember the works of the Lord; surely I will remember Your wonders of old. I will also meditate on all Your work, and talk of Your deeds.' He then talked about some of his own experiences, his testimony and how in London, England, at Holy Trinity Brompton he received a touch from God, when Sandy Millar (the vicar) prayed for him and he slid onto the floor and stayed there for some time being refreshed by the Lord.

At Brownsville on the day of the outpouring, Steve Hill proclaimed that God was going to do something special, having Divine assurance that the Holy Spirit was going to turn up, stating "...Every person who is dry will be drenched by rain." At the end of the service he gave an altar call and six people came forward. Steve Hill then focused on the remainder of the congregation and shared about what he saw and participated in Argentina and the fact that he did not realise he was so dry until God came and soaked him. Steve Hill asked those who needed more of God to come to the front and about one thousand did – half the congregation! In quick succession, Steve Hill, followed by Pastor Kilpatrick, began laying his hands on people, shouting single words as prayer commands, from one who was intimate with the Holy Spirit and obeyed His voice: "Jesus!" "Now!" "Fire!" and "More!" and the majority of people just collapsed to the floor under the power of God. This scene would be repeated as the evangelist who came with only five sermons was asked to preach in the evening service and continued to preach for four nights a week for the next five years! Within a few minutes, Pastor Kilpatrick who was up on the platform was Divinely touched by the Holy Spirit (without the laying on of hands) and collapsed to the floor (being uneasy on his feet – Who can stand in the presence of God?) and was in a wheel chair for the next few days. When Kilpatrick's flock saw their pastor on the floor, then they knew that God was in the house, as this was so out-of-character.

"Prior to the revival, the Brownsville Church was quite conservative" said Dr. Michael Brown, the resident theologian who joined the team in 1996. If people began to dance, and there was never many, Pastor Kilpatrick would look at the ushers and they would tell them to stop. "The church was healthy" Brown stated, and that "before the revival eighty percent of church members tithed."[1]

During the revival, thousands of people would turn up for the Tuesday night prayer meeting as the sanctuary was spiritually cleansed for the new week's meetings which started on Wednesday evening. Some people queued at 4:30am for the 7pm service. In July 1997, I saw crowds hundreds of metres long, two to four people thick in the mid afternoon summer heat of 35 centigrade. Security guards were employed to help assist in people management (and general security), so as not to cause chaos in the rundown community and there was a big car park to look after. One security guard stated that he had seen 8,000 people in the queue one day and had to turn hundreds away after all the overflow rooms and corridors were full![2]

Night after night as the doors were opened at 6pm (one hour before the service), people eager for God would cram into the 2,100-seat church sanctuary, once that was filled, people would file into the other buildings which could seat around seven hundred (a slightly larger building was built in 1997); people were also in the choir room, other overflow rooms and even in the corridors as speakers were located throughout the complex, even in the toilets – there was nowhere to hide! Services lasted around four hours with an eight-minute break after worship.

When I visited in the summer of 1997, you were not permitted to enter with bags; this was probably because on one Saturday night, a toxic gas bomb was ignited. A bomb of the same time was also let off at a nearby grocery shop and those who breathed in the fumes became very ill, though none at the church were injured.[3]

Lindell Cooley led the worship for around two hours while heaven and earth met as people sung glorious tribute to the Lamb that was slain and worshipped God. The congregation were accompanied by the ten-member praise-band and the one hundred and fifty purpled robed, yellow neck-clad choir. Often Steve Hill, John Kilpatrick or Dr. Michael Brown would speak, give a testimony and address different issues, whilst frequently teaching on past revivals, before the preaching commenced under Steve Hill. The leadership frequently stated from the front, that many people had so called 'words from the Lord' for the church, and that if they did, they were to submit it in writing, with a covering A4 letter from their pastor. This had to state their commitment to their home church, references to their lifestyle and that they regularly tithed, otherwise the Brownsville leadership would not be able to take them seriously.

By July 1997, over 300,000 people had responded to the call of salvation (and got right with God) and 1.7 million people from all sorts of social and economical backgrounds had visited from around the globe. They came to witness, to be a part of, to see the presence of God manifest and to get a fresh touch of fire. By the close of the millennium over 3.5 million people had visited Brownsville, and multitudes had taken fresh fire to their home churches and glowing reports of what had happened to them. In 1998 I met a young man at a Christian camp who a year previously, as a backslider visited Brownsville Church, got right with God and was still on fire for the Lord.

Steve Hill never stepped into the pulpit without the intercessory team praying over him first. Pastor Kilpatrick in the foreword to *Cross Pollination* wrote: 'The Brownsville Revival can be summed up in one word: souls. Yes, backsliders are coming back to God, but many thousands of first-time converts also come running to the mercy seat nightly. Thanks be to God for Lila Turhune [coordinator of the Intercessory Prayer Department] and her skilled army of intercessors that stay in the trenches to sigh and cry for all the abominations that are done in the midst thereof [see Ezekiel 9:3-4].'[4]

When it came to the reading from the Holy Bible (the main passage for his sermon) Steve Hill asked everybody to stand out of respect for the Word of God. Often Steve Hill would say, "Many of you go to Disney Land and spend several hours queuing for a ride, so there is no reason why you can't stand for the reading of the Word." Hill, for four nights a week (Wednesday to Saturday) would preach an uncompromising message of holiness and repentance – "Get the sin out of your life, embrace the cross, look to Jesus and call upon Him." Some of Steve Hill's revival sermons have been published in *White Cane Religion* (1997) and *The God Mockers* (1997).

Steve Hill would always use props in his sermons and it was different each night. Some of the more notable were a coffin, a tombstone, shackles, a bed of affliction and enlarged playing cards. One night he preached on the blind leading the blind, 'White Cane Religion' and wore dark glasses, held a white stick and was tapping his way around the stage. On another night, the lights were dimmed as his wife, wearing a wedding dress marched to the front. One evening very late into the altar call, Steve Hill felt prompted by God to ask one of the musicians to play a military tune, similar to a bugle call, to which military persons came to the front at the last stages of the altar call.

Since the summer of 1995, Charity James (who was just fourteen years old) sung, "Run to the Mercy Seat" at every altar call as hundreds of people ran to the front whilst Steve Hill called the people to get right with God, to repent, to cry out to Him for mercy. Many a repentant soul cried, wailed and moaned in deep repentance, being remorseful and full of grief; for numerous sinners tears flowed copiously as both children and adults alike, called upon the risen Saviour, Jesus Christ. For me, it was the most eerie sound I have ever heard and have never before or since heard repentance like it and the sight was incredible to behold. When people repent like what I saw and heard, they get well and truly saved, as those who have been forgiven more, love more (Luke 7:47).

At the end of the service, anybody could go forward for prayer and thousands would. There were numerous helpers and some strong catchers as most people hit the deck after being prayed for within a few seconds. Many people shook whilst under the power of God, and almost everybody on the floor were covered with modesty blankets, to keep people decent, both men and women. Frequently, before ministry time, the leadership would address the issue of women dressing like prostitutes and that it was not helpful for anybody – especially as they would probably end up slain under the power of the Holy Spirit. They would also state that they were not talking to new Christians (as it does take time to buy a new wardrobe), but to those who should know better, being older in the faith. The scene was frequently like a close combat battle zone as hundreds were touched by God. Many appeared to be in a coma and lay on the floor motionless for hours (as issues were being dealt with by the Holy Spirit), whilst others would twitch and their closed eyelids would move, some were healed, others had visions and revelations and some had to be carried out in the early hours and driven to their hotels! The hotel staff in and around the locality got very used to these scenes and after a while quickly realised where their guests had been and it was all very normal!

Finances

Pastor Kilpatrick would always take the Sunday morning service and at the end of the meeting he would always pray a blessing over the congregation. As in most churches an offering was taken (of which they had about twenty large copper offering plates). They told the visitors not to put their tithe into this offering as it would in affect be a curse. They stated that all tithes should go to your home church [unless directed by God otherwise], but they would accept any offerings and stated that the revival was expensive to maintain.

The *Pensacola News Journal* for November 1997 reported that the Brownsville Church had 107 paid church employees (including security guards, secretaries, crèche staff etc.) and their wage bill exceeded one million dollars annually. At different meetings they would take love offerings for different members of the Brownsville team. Dr. Michael Brown in 1997 said, "One of the strengths of the revival is that people have a heart to serve." There were lots of voluntary workers, the choir, ushers and those who served at the sales tables.

Nearing the end of the revival, the Destiny Image *Digest,* a quarterly magazine (Vol. 5 No. 1) reported that the toilet paper and cleaning supplies have to be dropped off weekly in large truck, with a $2,000 bill (approximately £1,250). 'Rent-a-cops show up for duty in your parking lot almost every night of the week to handle security and parking' whilst 'secretarial and administrative staff…deal with the hundreds of calls a day from nearly every continent that bombard eight overworked incoming phone lines.'[5]

Opposition

As in all revivals, many people spoke against this move of God, whilst other churches in the locality and beyond embraced it and saw the fire of God move in their church. About twenty-five members of the Brownsville church left, as it upset their weekly routine.

One person from the UK watched one Brownsville video and concluded that the Brownsville Revival was not of God. He wrote a booklet (which was on sale in my local Christian bookshop) describing his views having never even visited the Brownsville church! Another author in April 1997, spoke on *Larry King Live*, saying that spiritual deception was not exclusive to cults but could be found in mainstream Christian churches like Brownsville who practiced 'psychosocial manipulation' and 'altered states of consciousness.' He had just written a book on counterfeit revivals and vocally stated that Brownsville was a part of that.[6] Members of another church in the immediate area, also thought that the Brownsville Revival was not from God and had nothing good to say about it, yet that church was only a little over ten percent full. I visited this church on a Sunday evening (a night that Brownsville had off) and they gave you "that look" when you replied to their question, "What are you doing in Pensacola – on holiday?" and made a few negative comments. Jealousy (as well as ignorance) is a dangerous thing (see Acts 13:44-45). Several people over the years have shared their opinions and told me why the Brownsville Revival was not from God (and never in a polite concerned manner) though they never visited the place or researched the facts for themselves. It was at my visit to the Brownsville Revival that I received my call to Bible College, which flowed into full-time ministry. If I had not been obedient to the Divine call then life would be quite different now and my series of revival books would not have been written. As Dr. Michael Brown said, "The Brownsville experience is not so that you have a story to tell in ten years from now. This is so you can be spiritually launched into orbit."[7] And that was true for me, glory to God.

Warnings and Observations

Managing a revival is not an easy task. "Bright lights attract bugs" as Steve Hill used to say "and they're probably from your church!" – As in an age of instant media, news spreads fast and Brownsville became a "mecca" for a few million people. All of whom had various reasons and motives for attending and not all of it was pure or honourable. I was quite taken aback, when just before the service started they announced not to leave valuables unattended (e.g. purses or handbags – normal bags and cameras were not permitted into the church sanctuary), as they have been stolen in the past, especially during the time of ministry when everybody is moving about.

On at least one night at which I was present, members from another church in the locality placed leaflets on those who had been slain in the Spirit, stating how foolish they looked. This was also addressed by Steve Hill the following night, not to mock what God, and he warned, "Don't you dare!"

During the revival, Pastor Kilpatrick continually prayed, "Lord please give me wisdom to pastor this thing. Lord, I don't want to be so lenient that I let anything in, but Lord I don't want to be so hard either that I don't let what You're trying to do in – God please give me wisdom. Holy Spirit, help me to walk humbly before You. Holy Spirit, help me to keep my mind on the Lord and to keep my eyes on the Lord, and Holy Spirit, help me not to get distracted with things, where I begin to let the embers grow dim and cold in my life, and Lord, help me not to let the fire go out in this church; Lord, help me…"[8]

The Brownsville Revival had Several Unique Features
1. It is the longest running revival in America in a single location (a church) for the past two (if not three) centuries.
2. Every service was recorded, and as far as I am aware, it is the first time in history that the start of revival and the

continuance of it have been captured on film (video) in its entirety. During the revival, videos and audio tapes of the services were sold from the church and its website.

3. There was a break in meetings from December 1996 until January 1997 (of about two weeks) to give the church workers and volunteers a much needed rest. The leadership team knew that the revival would continue until the year 2000![9] Steve Hill moved to Dallas, Texas in June 2000 (though he did return to preach on occasions over the next four years) whilst John Kilpatrick resigned as senior pastor in 2003.

4. The Brownsville Church came out of the revival in debt (a first) – $9.5 million by June 2006, though this was largely due to the construction of a building to accommodate the crowds.

Fruit of the Revival

Billionaires attended the Brownsville meetings, as did prostitutes, the homeless, young and old, singles, couples, divorcees, pastors, church workers, atheists, murderers, backsliders, homosexuals, witches, warlocks and burnt-out discouraged Christians. Literally a few million visitors were touched (see Appendix D) and 100,000s were transformed, whilst others mocked this revival and said God was not in it.

Steve Hill often said, "Opinions are like trash cans everyone's got them, and most of them stink!" But the results of the fruit of these individuals' lives speak for themselves, the drug addicts were set free, backsliders left their ways of sin for holiness, marriages and broken relationships were restored, restitutions were made and a few hundred thousand were converted and there were also documented cases of healing!

The Brownsville School of Ministry (BSM) began in January 1997, for those who felt called into Christian ministry or for those who needed some practical biblical training. Within a few years, a few thousand have fanned throughout the world as witnesses for Jesus Christ and been fire-starters in their own churches. The *Pensacola News Journal* for November 1997 stated that there were 507 students attending BSM, 120 of which lived on campus. By autumn of 2000, there were 1,000 students at BSM so reported *Charisma* magazine (June 2005).

In July 1997, youth pastor, Richard Crisco held Brownsville's first annual Youth Conference and in the same year, Pastor Kilpatrick held the first annual Pastor's Conference. In 1998, Lidell Cooley held Brownsville's first Worship Conference. Beginning in 1997, senior members of Brownsville Church held

Awake America rallies in different cities of America (Dallas, Toledo, Birmingham, Memphis etc.) which was their way of responding to the numerous invitations they had to decline. Steve Hill would preach, give an altar call and thousands of people would respond, if not tens of thousands during the near dozen rallies they held in 1997 and 1998.

One pastor in the area had lunch with two of the bar owners in the locality. They told him that business has never been worse and half of their former clients were sitting in his church on a Sunday morning!

The Brownsville Revival was also instrumental in the Smithton outpouring (1996-2001), where 250,000 people from sixty nations visited a small farm town (population of just 532) in Smithton, Missouri, USA. This revival is documented in *I saw the Smithton Outpouring* by Ron McGatlin (2002).

The Youth

Dr. Michael Brown stated that the *Pensacola News Journal* for the 3 January 1997 reported that juvenile crime all over Florida rose one percent in 1996 and had been rocketing in the county, in some places at fifteen percent on the preceding year, but in this county, it dropped thirteen percent. The county Superintendent of Schools, a man who was not associated with Brownsville in mid-1997 approved a request from the Gideons to hand out Bibles before and after class at the public schools, from those in the fifth grade up to the twelfth.

Before the revival, only three out of the thirty-two junior high schools in the area had Christian Unions. Within two years, they all had them, some of which were 250 strong! Students in class would be touched by the Holy Spirit and collapse on the floor and many of the schools had separate rooms where these pupils could be placed. Countless testimonies of people poured in over the years and the healing power of God was very evident.

Richard Crisco, Brownsville youth pastor wrote *It's Time – Passing Revival to the Next Generation* (1997) where he states: 'It is time to stop entertaining youth and start training an army. This generation is bored with pizza parties and amusement park trips. It's time we resurrect them to the call of God upon their lives! It's time to pass on the power, purpose, and passion found in Jesus Christ to the next generation!'

Richard Crisco for many years tried to get to meet many of the school's principals in the locality but to no avail. Prior to the revival, the Brownsville Church had one hundred youth, within two years they had five hundred attending and after a process of discipleship found that after two years ninety percent of youth converts were still going on with the Lord.

Soon, school principals started to phone up Richard Crisco and invite him out for lunch, after the third time this had happened the principal explained that the administrators and the principals of the different schools had come together and informally decided that they need to seize this opportunity. Richard Crisco was asked to hold Youth Rallies on a Tuesday night every month in a different public school. The principals told him that they would announce that the Brownsville youth team would be in on a certain date.

At one Youth Rally, seventy people were converted. The sports coach had a list of the ten worse sinners; promiscuous girls, heavy drug users and prideful sports stars and all ten had been converted! Dr. Michael Brown retelling the story said, "He [the coach] was in a state of shock." At one school, some students decided to have a prayer and praise time during break and the Holy Spirit came and prostrated one of the fourteen year old boys. His mates carried him to his typing class and the teacher was not amused. She asked two boys (non-Christians) to carry their classmate to the principal's office. As they were doing this the power of God hit them! Dr. Brown went on to say that different principals phoned up Brownsville Church asking them what to do. Whilst some Christians phoned up Brownville and were "flipping out" because they heard that people were shaking and falling over at school, wanting to know if it was true. But as Dr. Brown stated, when these same kids were going into school carrying guns, dressing like prostitutes, guys with multi-coloured hair, cussing at the teachers, getting kicked out of school, séances in the hallways, pornography in kids lockers, gangs; these concerned Christians were not getting worked up about it, some of whom were their own children. "You know what's nice" said Dr. Brown, "God knows how to make Himself real to a young person."

Dr. Michael Brown was approached by a cynic who asked about the youth, whether or not 'it is possible that some of them are getting in the flesh?' His reply was, "I'm sure it's possible that some of them are getting in the flesh, just as I'm very sure it's probable that ninety-nine percent of people sitting in dead churches are in the flesh the whole time."

Shillong Revival (2006-2007)

Welsh missionaries first arrived in the Indian state of Mizoram in 1840 and continued arriving until 1960; bringing the Good News of the Gospel of Jesus Christ. In 2006, eighty percent of the state's population were Christians whilst missionaries from Mizoram (and others states of India and parts of Asia) are now missionaries in Wales![1] *Operation World – 21st Century Edition* states that most Christians in Mizoram are either Presbyterian or Baptist and that 'awakenings and revivals in recent years have dynamized the church and transformed society.' Over 2,000 missionaries have been raised up and the state is also the most literate and well-educated in India.

The Khasi Hills Revival (1905-1906) in India saw 8,200 former Hindu's baptised within two years. See *The Revival in the Khasia Hills* by Mrs John Roberts (1906). Rev. Vanlalchhuanawma, an expert in the history of revivals, speaking to the BBC news website in October 2006 said, "The revival in 1906 gave help to the evangelical works of Welsh missionaries in both [the states of] Meghalaya and Mizoram."

Meghalaya, is known as 'Scotland of the East' and is a hill town in the north eastern part of India with Shillong as its capital. Meghalaya covers an area of approximately 300 kilometres in length and about 100 kilometres in breadth. It is surrounded by Assam on the north and east and by Bangladesh on the south and west. The Khasis, Jaintias and Garos are the main tribes of Meghalaya.[2]

Reuben Pradhan wrote: 'In the year 2003, the Khasi Jaintia Presbyterian Synod (West) had their first gathering in a village called Mawkyrwat in the West Khasi Hills of Meghalaya. In this meeting it was decided to hold an ongoing chain-prayer movement for God to bring revival in the land once again as it happened a hundred years ago during 1905-06. As such, it was also decided that the doors of the chapels would remain open every morning for believers to gather for prayers. It was acknowledged by all that there was a major spiritual decline in the church and in the moral lifestyle of the people in general. This made the church to turn to the Lord in expectancy that He would send a fresh wave of renewal and transformation once again.'[3]

I am much indebted to Barkos Warjri (a Khasi who lived in Bangalore, until returning to his homeland in March 2007), for the majority of the facts about the Shillong Revival. He has received many reports from family and friends and was able to visit his homeland in late December 2006 until January 2007 under arrangement from the Mairang Presbytery, when he met many of those involved in the revival and those who have been transformed by the Holy Spirit who came in revival power.

Shillong's first revival broke out on the 1 April 1906. A century later, revival burst forth on Saturday the 22 April 2006 amongst a huge number of people in Mairang, the place where the 1906 Assembly took place. In April 2006, hundreds of delegates were attending the afternoon service of the Revival Centenary commemoration, whilst a minimum of 150,000 people (with reports of up to 300,000) sat outside on the huge lawns of the Mairang Presbyterian Church. The Holy Spirit came 'in such a powerful way' that the delegates continued to sing and pray for hours, unmoved, in driving rain which continued for about half an hour, oblivious to the elements.

Reuben Pradhan wrote: 'We watched on a local TV news how the people drenched in the rain were crying out to God and repenting of their sins, while many were shaking with the power of God. The heavy downpour seemed to symbolize the outpouring of the promised Latter Rain.'

Barkos Warjri wrote: 'The revival is taking place in an area of about 14,000 square kilometres and has affected thousands of local churches. The churches affected have been almost entirely Presbyterian but a few other denominations have been touched.' The revival has even touched some churches in the adjoining state of Mizoram.

'Many people, especially children have been miraculously converted without any preaching, but simply by the conviction of the Holy Spirit. Miraculous events have [also] taken place in many of the churches with thousands of children throughout the hills seeing visions of God, Jesus Christ, heaven, hell, resulting in convictions of these children, their relatives or the churches concerned. Families and whole communities have been transformed.' The Holy Spirit even descended on 'all schools [in the area] be they state schools, church schools, or private schools [and on a college of more than two thousand pupils!] For several of the schools, regular classes were disrupted. Children from the age of about five expressed strong desires to be in church or simply to sing praises to God and pray.' At one state school, the Holy Spirit descended and the effect on the teenagers, all of whom were in their smart school uniforms was caught on video, I have seen the footage. Some were worshiping the Lord, sitting on the desks, kneeling or standing, whilst others were crying, still others were in prayer, and some were even being carried out of the classrooms in what I would call a spiritual comatose state, being under the power of the Holy Spirit.

Reuben Pradhan wrote: 'Then in the days that followed [the outbreak of the revival] news began to pour in that it was happening in different places but largely amongst the Presbyterians and that especially among the younger generation. Then we heard that students in a school in Silchar in Assam were experiencing the outpouring of the Holy Spirit. The school authorities not being able to rule out the fact actually had those students [who were in a spiritual comatose state] taken to a hospital! Some people and pastors from Shillong visited that place while some learned about it when they were watching a national cable news channel based in Delhi. Not being able to ascertain this strange phenomenon the channel carried the news headline calling it a "Mass Hysteria". Of late [by 1 Sept 2006] such occurrences is happening not only among Christians gathered in church buildings but also spreading among students in schools.'

In the beginning of October 2006, the BBC news website reported of the religious fervour at Meghalaya. Rev. Laldawngliana, a spokesman for the Presbyterian Church of India in Shillong said, "The Holy Spirit is here to reawaken people." In an email in February 2007, Barkos Warjri wrote: 'The Presbyterian Church in the Khasi and Jaintia Hills, which is the body called the Assembly has officially accepted the revival as the work of God and an answer to prayers.' But 'some pastors within the Presbyterian Church have not accepted this as the work of God. Where the pastor does not accept there is a quenching, but this is not so in all such local churches. There are places where the desire of the congregation seems to overwhelm the reluctance of the leader (strange but true). The numbers of such pastors is however small.

'Many of the local churches are open everyday for services, e.g. the Laban Church, and the Jaiaw Church, to name two in the capital city of Shillong. Some churches have reduced services to about four days a week' but 'almost all churches have revival meetings / services every evening.' The majority of the converts of the revival are mainly from the traditional 'Khasi' religion. Some people have classified this religion as Hindu but many do not accept it as such but rather as a separate 'Khasi' belief system (since Hinduism is a broad category however it can include such groups too). The Khasi religion however does not have the same characteristics as that of Hinduism and so should be correctly be classified as different; as one example it involves no idol worship. There are also converts from among the Hindus and there are reports of some Muslim converting to Christ. During the revival there have been numerous acts of spontaneous acts of public confession and restitution, forgiveness and confession of financial misdeeds.

On the 5 September 2006, at the Malki Presbyterian Church, Shillong, a plain wooden cross, a little less than three feet high, which is located on the wall behind the pulpit began to glow and an image of Jesus Christ could be seen. Even the BBC website reported on this strange event which lasted until November 2006. Thousands flocked to see it, Christians and non-Christians, and 24-hour worship (to the Lord) carried on at the church for days. Watching a video clip online, the Malki Church, a traditional stone church building with a high ceiling was jam packed with at least a thousand worshippers, with many more outside. But, four months later, the Malki Church, where Barkos Warjri grew up, and where the most miraculous manifestations occurred still held daily meetings, but, for some unbeknown reason they were lifeless and very poorly attended.

On Thursday, 19 October 2006, Khlainbor Lyngdoh, a middle-aged man, an evangelist, (with the gift of healing) who holds a secular job in the Government of Meghalaya went to Smit to give a Bible Study. A young girl from the Sohra area who had been seeing miraculous visions had come to meet him that day. She went along with him to the Bible study.

Barkos Warjri, received the following report from his family and friends and on the 21 October 2006 and takes up the story. He wrote: 'Bible studies are no longer small group meetings in the Khasi and Jaintia Hills these days. They are more like crusades. [On Thursday the 19 October 2006] the church building was full and so were the church lawns.' The young girl from the Sohra area had given her testimony, and said that God would do wonderful things that night. 'God had been doing so many wonderful things that people half expected what would happen. That night, however, it was something a bit beyond the ordinarily wonderful things they had been used to. It was not simply a response to God's word or miraculous visions (which are usually poured out to dozens of children nowadays). [The] heavens would open.'

The meeting concluded at about 9pm, the congregation had been singing, 'Showers of Blessing' and were beginning to leave; Khlainbor Lyngdoh also known as *Bah Khlain was walking towards his car. *'Bah' is the equivalent of 'Mr' and is used to address a male respectfully, especially, but not exclusively, used when addressing an older man. 'There was a noise and commotion outside. The young girl who had received many visions from the Lord said, "Let's go out, God is going to show something to you." 'The people outside had seen a bright light like lightning. The heavens towards the north seem to part and some saw what looked like hills, and then a rainbow (it was 9pm at night). Then there were screams and shouts like, "Here, here," "There, on the right," "Look there on the left." There were angels all around! Some fell down in fear or in shock. Some walking on the road dropped to their knees...'

Bah Khlain used his mobile video phone camera to capture the moving images of the angels against a dark sky (probably a world first!), with some children in the foreground. Clifford Kharsyntiew and Ricky Syngkon were also present as were hundreds of other people. Bah Ricky is a lecturer in the Commerce Department of the North Eastern Hill University, Shillong. Bah Clifford is a businessman, whom God had miraculous healed just a few weeks before. He had previously been on drugs and alcohol which not only ruined his life, but his business as well. On the 13 February 2005, a truck ran over him, crushing his lumber vertebrae in his spine. Even the renowned CMC Vellore hospital said nothing could be done. He could however hobble around a little. In April 2006 he went into a coma, when he awoke he was paralysed and completely bed-ridden. Before his maid / care-worker left, she recommended that he should call upon Jesus and he did. In the afternoon his sister, Audrey, who had not been in touch with him for months, called and told him about Bah Khlain who had the gift of healing. The next day Bah Khlain came with Ricky Syngkon and Audrey. They prayed over him and gave him a spoon of anointed oil, Clifford immediately got up. That evening Clifford went out with his friends and returned to his old habits. The next morning he awoke and found himself paralysed! He phoned Bah Klain who said, "Your body can be healed, but it is your spirit that needs to be healed first." For two months Clifford studied the Bible. On the 28 of June 2006, Bah Khlain prayed again, gave him the anointed oil and the man was immediately raised from the sick bed! The word he received from God was, "It is easy for Me to heal you. But will you serve Me?"[4]

Bah Clifford and Bah Ricky said that the hymn being sung outside the church was 'Showers of Blessing' but the phone recorded the song, 'The Angels are Singing' a song which became very popular during the revival. Barkos Warjri wrote: 'The recording had only male voices singing, and the voices of children shouting about the angels in the background. In reality there were many children singing 'Showers of Blessing' in the church. I vouch for the fact that only male voices can be heard singing on the video recording.'

On the 2 January 2007, in Shillong, Barkos Warjri interviewed Bah Khlain, Bah Ricky, and Bah Clifford and got first hand accounts of what happened. He also viewed the footage from the mobile phone and a month later, this footage was emailed to me and I viewed it for myself, the screen was tiny on the computer, but white flashy objects, (the angels) could be seen with children in the foreground. Barkos Warjri first heard about the angel incident from his family and friends, a little more than an hour after it occurred. He phoned up Bah Khlain the following day and wrote: 'A big angel flashed right in the path of the lens.' (After the personal interview in January 2007, he wrote: 'In fact they were all big but the one who came close appeared big, naturally. Clifford even felt the angel brush the side of his face'). 'My cousins,' continued Barkos Warjri 'who saw the picture on the screen last night [the day after it was filmed] were still shaken even two hours later. They said they could see the wings and the vague shape of a body. Angels are something we read about and hear of. Not beings we actually expect to see...'

Both Bah Khlain and Bah Ricky work together as a ministry team, praying for peoples needs and have seen wonderful healings and deliverances (from demons) in the mighty name of Jesus. They always use oil, to anoint the person in the name of the Lord (Mark 6:13) and prescribe some to be drunk, which they place in little bottles and since the revival broke out they purchased the oil in ten litre containers and several of them at a time! Bah Khlain began his healing ministry ten years ago, when his children were young, he began to anoint them with oil and pray and they got healed immediately. 'Today people come from all over Meghalaya, Mizoram, and Nagaland to get prayer. No problem is too big! Cancer, demon possession, kidney failure, tumours are all dealt with. He gives the sick two small bottles of oil. One is meant for drinking and the other for applying on the body.'[5]

Barkos Warjri after interviewing various people about that special night wrote: 'A bright sword was seen by some and some others a bright cross. A senior pastor married to my aunt, came out of the church building. He had been sceptical during the initial periods of the revival. "What do you think of this?" I ventured. "Think of what?" he asked, "I saw it with my own eyes! I saw the northern sky towards the Himalayas, and there was this bright cross, clear and bright up there. I was not alone! Several of us saw. Then I saw another cross, closer." ' Barkos Warjri continued in his report: 'I had recently had a long conversation with him when I visited Shillong [in January 2007]. I sensed now he was speaking with the excitement of one who was a part of something big happening, and I could no longer trace any scepticism in his words. However, I could not resist probing a little more. Knowing him to be a thinking pastor, an intelligent and bright student, I asked how this fitted in to his theology. "Do you remember what Joel said? What is written there is happening. These are miracles," he said, "When God does miracles how can we explain? These are beyond human explanations. I have seen and I believe." I remembered those who do not see and yet believe. I had spoken to three eyewitnesses. They were excited, but how much can they be excited when God seems to be literally pouring out His Spirit all around?'

'Two weeks ago the same pastor had met a young boy of seven in a remote village. He had become unconscious [in a comatose state] one day and had a vision. When he woke up the pastor asked him what happened. He said he had been to heaven, and as with many children who had visions of heaven or Jesus, he said that he did not want to return. Jesus had told him that he had to return for now and the boy had reluctantly found himself in the company of ordinary humans like this pastor. When asked if he had anything to say to anyone, he simply said, "Read Matthew 3:2" [which reads 'Repent, for the kingdom of heaven is at hand!'] Children of seven do not normally think of such verses, and certainly not someone who could hardly read.'

National Highway 44 connects the states of Mizoram, Tripura, and the plains of Cachar to the rest of the country, through the Jaintia Hills and Khasi Hills of Meghalaya. An empty refrigerated truck was returning after delivering its load of fish from Andhra Pradesh, in Silchar. The driver, also from Andhra, stopped at Bapung, in the Jaintia Hills, that evening and heard singing from the Bapung Presbyterian Church. He was drawn by the singing into the church and joined in the worship even though he did not know the language and at the end of the service some of the counsellors from the church prayed with him (I believe he got converted).

Barkos Warjri and his wife Pauline, visited Mairang on 26 December 2006 on the arrangement of the Mairang Presbytery, and talked to pastors, church elders and to many children and young women. They then visited the Khasi and Jaintia Hills of Meghalaya and returned home a little over two weeks later. He wrote: 'My trip to my home [land] was most different, unlike any other visit, and it has given me another perspective of our God, a God whose love is greater than what I had understood earlier, immensely greater and one who longs to have us close to Him. I have also come back with a much clearer understanding of what Jesus meant when he said that the kingdom of God / heaven was of such (while talking of the little children). What starkly came out was the fact that the greatest impediment to the work of God is indeed human or worldly wisdom and learning.'

On the 18 January 2007, Bah Knight, an elder for fifty years at the Nongsawlia Presbyterian in Sohra and a few others visited Mawlynnong village which has been awarded the cleanest village in Asia. Bah Knight said that not only was the village clean, it had the highest literacy as well. The best news followed as he said to Barkos Warjri in a telephone interview, "New life has come here as well. Revival has broken out in the area in the Presbyterian churches as well as the CNI (Church of North India) churches in the area."[6]

Friday Lyngdoh, Minister with the Meghalaya Government, in January 2007 said that the changes in society were real. When asked if he had seen any of the big signs of the revival, like the glowing cross at Malki he replied, "No, I have not. But I have seen the street outside my house. The people who used to stand around in the dark – drunk and swearing – have reduced a lot. Many broken families have got together. Yes, many people have experienced change."[7]

At the end of Janaury 2007, the Presbyterian Synod met and decided to regularly pray for revival to break out in Wales, UK, like it had in Shillong. 'There is a sense of debt that Shillong owes to the Welsh who brought the revival fire to the Khasi and Jaintia hills.'[8]

By February 2007, there was no clear system for discipleship except in a few local churches. The Laban Church in Shillong had Tuesday and Thursday evening for Bible teaching (the subject at the beginning of February 2007 was the Second Coming). They also had some 'testimony evenings' but not on a regular weekly basis. In the last six months (spanning 2006-2007) they had had two weekend retreats. On Friday the 2 February till Saturday the third, about 1,000 people were in attendance on a weekend retreat. They were split into many groups, based largely on age & also gender for some sessions.

The main emphasis of the Shillong Revival was that 'the time is near' and the end of the age is drawing to a close before the Lord's return. Barkos Warjri wrote: 'A deacon from the Iewrynghep Presbyterian Church (near Mawlyngngot), in East Khasi Hills, had a vision in his bedroom one night, he saw a big angel about to blow the trumpet, but something made him pause and he dropped his arm. Almost all the children having received visions repeat this same message, the door is about to be locked, or the book is about to be closed.'

Father led to Repentance by his Young Daughter

Iba Warjri studies in Class Two even though she is already eight years old. Barkos Warjri first heard of her in October 2006 when he was told of a little girl who had a vision and when she woke up from her unconscious state she recounted her vision of the rapture, Jesus' return, the judgement and so on as if she had read the book of Daniel. Barkos met her along with his wife, on the 26 December 2006 at her village, Nongrim Sadew, about 25 kilometres from Shillong, and spoke to her and many others to verify the reports.

Barkos Warjri wrote: 'The last few days of August 2006 and the month of September run like a movie on perennial fast forward. The events moved so fast that normal life was thrown out of gear. School attendances were disrupted and churches were working overtime, many of them open 24 hours. The Presbyterian Church in the Khasi and Jaintia hills observed a 'Youth Week' during the week ending 2 September 2006 with the final day falling on Sunday 3 September 2006. On 2 September the Youth Week services were special. There was a tremendous outpouring of God's Spirit. Young men and women and children fell like ninepins as they were overcome by the sheer presence of God. Iba (the girl of eight) saw a vision of the end times and after that, one of the women in the church called out "Jesus, Jesus." Iba rushed out of the church building along with many others. When she looked at the moon, it looked like a cloud very near her. She saw an image of Jesus in the cloud and then it disappeared. The stars looked as if they were following the moon, which seemed to move very fast. She saw a crown and angels dressed in white. She saw God's glory but could not see His face, nor could she describe His majesty. She also saw her parents wearing crowns. She was so happy, she praised God and danced, in her own words, "like mad woman. I called all the men and children but I was scolded. I thought it was the last day, and that we would all be saved."

'An elderly lady, Kong Wello, who was present at the church that night told us that when Iba woke up she said that this was the last great revival and asked to speak to the four church elders. She told them that Jesus was coming soon and that He would first take up the dead and then the living and then 666 would rule. My wife asked Iba where she had heard such a thing before and Iba said she had known of no such thing' and was not that good at reading.

'Iba's mother told us that when she had the revelations that night her face was transformed. She is the least pretty of all the siblings but on that night she was radiant and bright and her voice was sure and clear. She normally cannot speak the standard Khasi language well, usually using her local dialect, but when she has a revelation she speaks fluent Khasi. It is evident that it is the Lord who gives her the words. But on that night it was not only Iba, several others had visions and most of them prayed for, and called, their loved ones to come to the church. Iba called for her father. Iba's father was from a Roman Catholic background and her mother was Presbyterian, but after they got married they had stopped attending church. Their children had no Christian teaching at home. Iba's father is not ashamed to speak of his past life. He said, "I have been a man who has been in the kingdom of the king of this earth. Why should I not tell the truth, frankly? I have been a notorious man. I liked to drink, yes; I usually take up to seven half bottles of my favourite whisky. I was not afraid of the police. I think they were afraid; they did not want to have a scrap with me. I am not a trouble maker but if someone starts making trouble, I do not hesitate to make the fire hotter. On the night of the 2 September 2006, I came back home drunk, and when one of the boys from the church came to tell me that my daughter was calling me, I was too drunk to comprehend what was happening. The next day, Sunday I was about to have my bath when I heard my daughters voice over the [church's] public address system. It was about 11am. Something strange happened. I felt as if my heart was stabbed. I could no longer have my bath. I put on my clothes again, slipped into a pair of slippers and rushed off to the church. I do not know what drove me there, but I could no longer remain still. As I entered the gate of the church I heard my daughter saying that her father was coming to church. I lurched to the main door and overcome by some kind of power I almost crawled towards the front of the church and knelt there. I saw my daughter there, her face radiant, and I just wanted to kneel down. I knew I was a sinner and I asked God for forgiveness. Believe me sir," he said, "from that day onwards I have not taken a single drop of alcohol." A few Sundays earlier the whole family had been baptised and become full members of the church.

'On that night as we were in the evening service we saw several children having visions. Iba also fell asleep. When she woke up she said that she had seen Jesus and as well [as] satan with four horns, and then another demon with seven horns, and than another big one with ten horns, and he then turned into a serpent. "I then saw angels singing and was led to heaven where I danced and sang. It was a beautiful place. There were brass and wind instruments. Then Jesus sent me to the pulpit to pray. He asked me to take off my shoes. I saw only His feet and His wounded hands." We saw her going to the pulpit and taking off her shoes in a semi-conscious state. She went to the pulpit twice and prayed there after which she woke up.

Another girl, Phibakyntiew Lyngdoh Nongbri, aged ten, also fell unconscious. We heard her speak in her trance and say, "I have reached, I have reached... The angels and trumpets. You must repent, you cannot go back again and again to the same things, it is no use." When she woke up she told us that Jesus had come to the church and when He came the church shone brightly and that He asked all to repent. There were lots of angels and they looked at the people and they sang and blew their trumpets, and birds were standing on the lectern and dancing. Barkos Warjri continued with his report: ' "They are very lovely birds," she said in her sleep, "I really like that, I really like that. I will stay here with Jesus. I will not go home. I will not stay in a world full of troubles." She smiled sweetly in her sleep and giggled as if she was playing, saying, "I will pluck that... I will take that (as if she was gathering fish in a net)... Oh the flowers are so lovely! I am so happy with Jesus...I have no worries (she chuckles), oh this pond is so beautiful and clean, the water is so sweet."

'Another girl prayed for herself in her trance, for her parents and her five siblings... Others in the church were identifying them for us [Barkos Warjri and associates] as the girl prayed. What had touched me deeply was the evident enthusiasm in the singing of many young boys and girls and the intensity of their prayers. I could see tears streaming on their faces as they cried to God. When they sang it was as if they were seeing something else as they raised their voices. There was no hesitation, they shouted out their praises.'

In May 2007, the webmaster of shillongrevival.com, Bert Cherian, informed me: 'The work in Shillong continues. The overt signs have come down, and in its place there is an atmosphere of holiness...'

In late July 2007, the fire of revival in the city of Shillong had greatly faded and was evidently winding down, though in the surrounding rural areas, many churches were still experiencing revival. Barkos Warjri in July 2007 wrote: 'I see clearly that the churches in the Khasi and Jaintia Hills, by and large, have not been ready for the new wine. The wineskins, in many places, have split open. Yet the encouragement is that there are many who remain, many who also intercede.'

In a strange twist, on the 3 September 2007, the cross at the Malki Presbyterian Church in Shillong began glowing again (though differently than in 2006) and thousands flocked there once again. The cross first glowed on the 5 September 2006 until November 2006 (see page 96), but since, this 'sign,' recommenced many initially believed that God had not finished with Shillong, though the revival had peaked months ago and was evidently winding down.[9]

Our Responsibility

*NO
Revival started
with Jesus, for
40 Days, & 10 days
with H. S.*

For the Church, revival began at Pentecost when the Holy Spirit was poured out and three thousand people were added to the body of Christ. In the Old Testament there were several noted revivals under different prophets, judges and kings when God's people returned to the Lord. Revival has always been a part of God's plan, to revive Christians and to convert and transform sinner's enmasse.

In this book, I have recorded just twelve revivals from the past 150 years as a means of encouragement, and also a challenge. What God has done, He can do again. The Holy Bible declares that God must be glorified (Leviticus 10:3); Jesus will return for His Bride, which will be without spot or wrinkle (Ephesians 5:27); God has no pleasure in the death of the wicked and desires all men to be saved (Ezekiel 18:23 and 1 Timothy 2:4). In times of revival, all these ideals (not Jesus' return) can find fulfillment – God is glorified amongst the heathen, Jesus is exalted, the Holy Spirit is given His rightful place within the Church; the Church is purged of its sin and gets itself right before a holy God; sinners come seeking the Saviour, backsliders are drawn back into the fold and communities can be transformed!

Rev. Duncan Campbell of the Lewis Revival (1949-1952) in Scotland, wrote: 'Let me say what I frequently say – that the God I believe in is a covenant-keeping God who is true to His engagements. 'If you will keep My commandments and execute My judgments, then will I do it!" (1 Kings 6:12).

Our covenant-keeping God has declared, "If My people who are called by My name will humble themselves and pray and seek My face and turn from their wicked ways, then I will hear from heaven, and will forgive their sin and heal their land" (2 Chronicles 7:14). 'God is not a man that He should lie...has He said, and will He not do it? Or has He spoken, and will He not make it good?' (Numbers 23:19).

God is not obligated to send revival if we have negated our responsibilities, which all revolves around living right before God and man (see Psalm 15, Psalm 24:3-6, Isaiah 58, Hosea 10:12 and Matthew 5:1-12), but as long as we do not fail to fulfill our part, then He will not fail to fulfill His. We must live holy lives. As the body of Christ, the Church, it is our individual and corporate responsibility to live holy God-glorifying lives so that we do not bring reproach to the name of Jesus Christ.

Revival is accomplished through God's sovereignty and man's fulfilled responsibility, (the Divine-human partnership) and is revealed in the fullness of time. All things are decreed in heaven (Psalm 119:89), but they have to be outworked on earth, practically through our prayers and intercession.

We need to plead God's covenant promises so that the Spirit will be poured out on those who are thirsty; for the floods to be poured out on our dry and barren land – so that the desert will bloom once again and God will be glorified amongst the nations.

A personal revival always precedes a local or national revival and every one of us is accountable to God. On the Judgment Day we will not only be accountable for what we said and did – but for what we did not say and did not do.

'Deliver those who are drawn towards death, and hold back those stumbling to slaughter. If you say, "Surely we did not know this," does not He who weighs the heart consider it? He who keeps your soul, does He not know it? And will He not render to each man according to his deeds?'
Proverbs 24:11-12.

'For I will pour water on him who is thirsty, and floods on the dry ground; I will pour My Spirit on your descendants, and My blessing on your offspring; they will spring up among the grass like willows by the watercourses' Isaiah 44:3-4.

Also by Mathew Backholer:

- *Revival Fires and Awakenings*
- *Understanding Revival and Addressing the Issues it Provokes*
- *Global Revival – Worldwide Outpourings*
- *How to Plan, Prepare and Successfully Complete your Short-term Mission*
- *Mission Preparation Training*

Available from: www.ByFaithBooks.co.uk

Appendix A

In early October 1857, a revival broke out in Hamilton, Ontario, Canada, which is known as Canada West. It began when Holiness Methodist preachers, Dr. Walter C. Palmer and his wife, Phoebe, began holding evangelistic campaigns.[1] The American revival affected four men in Kells to see the same blessing in their community which led to the Irish Revival (1859-1860) which encouraged others, that in turn spread and affected Scotland, Wales and England to pray and believe for revival which in turn went around the world resulting in a Great Awakening on a global scale.[2] In 1858, Sweden saw 200,000 conversions as revival touched them for two years. The heaven-sent blessing circled the globe as the news spread of this great awakening. In late 1859, revival broke out across India in what became known as the India Awakening, though the broadest work was seen in the South of India, and in this year was the beginning of the evangelisation of Brazil. In 1860, revival also broke out in Jamaica, in various towns and areas across the Cape Colony of South Africa (especially among the Dutch Reformed Church) and Shanghai, China.[3]

In October 1909, Bishop E. Graham Ingham, Home Secretary of the Church Missionary Society was in Tokyo, Japan at the Semi-Centennial Conference (1859-1909). Quoting, Rev. Dr. Imbrie of the American Presbyterian Mission he wrote that Japans past fifty years was divided into three periods and that the first stage was 'the period: of awakening...of reaction...of recovery...God was in the awakening.'[4]

In June 1865 Hudson Taylor, a missionary to China (who had been invalided home to England in 1860) whilst in Brighton was challenged and called by the Holy Spirit to start the China Inland Mission. He believed and prayed for twenty-four new workers, and was encouraged by the English Revival (1859-1860) – If God was pouring out his blessing on the homeland then He could bless China with missionaries! In England, Hudson Taylor spoke at different conferences and made appeals for missionaries – he got twenty-four and they sailed for China in May 1866.

Appendix B

In March 2001, the Ministry of Education of the Democratic People's Republic of Korea (DPRK) authorized the establishment of the Pyongyang University of Science and Technology (PUST) by the Northeast Asia Foundation for Education and Culture (NAFEC), a South Korean non-profit organization. On the 16 September 2009, the building dedication service for (PUST) was held. PUST is near the Daedong River area, where Robert J. Thomas was martyred in 1866 and has been built on the site of the former Thomas Memorial Church, which was destroyed under Communism.

Dr. James Chin-Kyung Kim, founding president and co-chairman of PUST wrote: 'While the skills to be taught are technical in nature, the spirit underlying this historic venture is unabashedly Christian. A century ago, the northern half of the Korean peninsula was steeped in Christian and modern influences, so much so that Pyongyang, its centre, was known throughout Western Christendom as "the Jerusalem of the East." God in

His Providence has granted us a second opportunity to teach modern subjects to new generations of young North Koreans to encourage them to become, once again, eager to learn and borrow from the outside world.'[5]

Appendix C

James A. Stewart ministered in and around Czecho-Slovakia, Poland and Hungary until the outbreak of World War II. He also saw revival in Bucharest, Rumania before the summer of 1939. He founded the European Evangelistic Crusade (1942) and preached in every country of Europe, except Albania, from the Norwegian Artic to Turkey. He began radio evangelism in 1949 when he purchased airtime on Radio Luxembourg (the strong long wave radio in Europe) with more than 80% of Europe as potential listeners. He later moved to North Carolina, America, (saw revival at a Bible Conference in North America) and wrote regular articles for Christian magazines throughout the world.

A biography of *James Stewart Missionary* by Ruth Stewart (his wife) was published in 1975. Chapter 8 covers their 'Love, Courtship and Marriage' (23 May 1938) which was all related to Budapest, Hungary during 1937-1938. James A. Stewart died in July 1975.

Appendix D

Dick Bernal is the senior pastor of Jubilee Christian Center in San Jose, California, a church of nearly 6,000 members. On the back cover of his book *Storming Hell's Brazen Gates* (1997) it states: 'Originally printed in 1988 *Storming Hell's Brazen Gates* was a catalyst in sparking one of the greatest revivals in modern times – the great Florida revival at the Assembly of God. The principles of this book [spiritual warfare] helped open the skies over the Pensacola area...a tremendous outpouring.'

J. Lee Grady visited the Brownsville Revival in March 1996 and again in July 1996. In the foreword to *Time To Weep – Discover the Power of Repentance that Brings Revival* by Stephen Hill (1996) he wrote: 'I knew this was genuine revival not just because I felt the holiness of God in the room, or because people were literally convulsing as they fell to their knees in front of the podium. I knew because my own heart was laid bare by an invisible sword as Steve humbly shared from the Scriptures. His message was not hype; it wasn't manipulating people with his delivery. His words were simply bathed in God's power, and it melted all human resistance. Including mine.'

Derek and Ruth Prince visited the Brownsville Revival in February 1997. In the introduction to *The Pursuit of Revival – Igniting a Passionate Hunger for More of God* by Stephen Hill (1997) he wrote: 'I saw in the leadership there, a willingness to make room for the Holy Spirit. Even though some of the manifestations that came were very unexpected, unusual, and could be interpreted as somewhat undignified, nevertheless, they yielded to the Holy Spirit. Jesus was central, there was no focus on any human personality. He was the Alpha and the Omega – it all revolved around Him.'

Sources and Notes

Prayer Meeting Revival 1857-1859

1. *Narrative of Remarkable Conversion and Revival Incidents* (NRCRI) – *Great Awakening of 1857-'8* by William C. Conant, Derby & Jackson, 1859, pp.412 & 415.
2. Ibid, page 420.   3. Ibid, page 357.
4. *Revival Times in America* by Fred W. Hoffman, W. A. Wilde Company, 1956, pages 108-109.
5. Ibid, p.111 & (NRCRI) – *Great Awakening of 1857-'8* – Conant, pp.361-362.
6. *The Half Can Never Be Told*, World Wide Revival Prayer Movement (WWRPM), 1927, page 24.   7. Ibid, page 32.
8. *The Second Evangelical Awakening* by J. Edwin Orr, Marshall, Morgan & Scott, 1949, 1955 abridged edition, pages 13-14.
9. (NRCRI) – *Great Awakening of 1857-'8* by William C. Conant, page 380.
10. *Handbook of Revivals* by Henry C. Fish, 1874, pages 69-70.
11. *When the Fire Fell* by George T.B. Davis, Schmul Publishers undated, pp.28-29.
12. *The Half Can Never Be Told*, WWRPM, 1927, pages 54-55.
13. *Great Revivals* by Colin Whittaker, Marshall, Morgan & Scott, 1984, pp.73-74.
14. *Old Time Revivals* by John Shearer, Pickering & Inglis, undated, page 85.
15. *America's Great Revivals* (no named author) Bethany House Publishers, no date, c.2000, page 91.
16. *Life of Dr. Talmage*, W. Percy Hicks, The Christian Herald, 1902, pp.51-57 & 70.
17. *Good News in Bad Times* by J. Edwin Orr, Zondervan Publishing House, 1953, pages 19-20.
18. *A Narrative of The Great Revival which Prevailed in the Southern Armies* by William W. Bennett, 1876, page iv.

Gold Coast Revival 1875-1878

1. *Thomas Birch Freeman, Missionary Pioneer to Ashanti, Dahomey & Egba* by J. Milum, London, S. W. Partridge & Co., 1894, chapters one and two and pp.120-130.
2. Ibid pages 9-31, 79, 138-140 and 156.   3. Ibid, pages 35-37 and 141-143.
4. Ibid, pages 144-149.   5. Ibid, pages 33-34.   6. Ibid, pages 151, 157.

Azusa Street Revival 1906-1909

1. *Another Wave of Revival* by Frank Bartleman, 1962 (Voice Christians Publication, Inc. under the title *Another Waves Rolls In – Additions and Revision*), 1982, Whitaker House, some factual extracts from chapter one.
2. *God's Generals* by Robert Liardon, Albury Publishing, 1996, pages 145-148.
3. *Another Wave of Revival* by Frank Bartleman, 1962, 1982, Whitaker House, pages 47-48 and 51.   4. Ibid, pages 56-58 and 61-62.   5. Ibid, page 125.
6. Revival in the Morning by Dale Gentry, Canaan's Promise, 1996, page 50.
7. *Azusa Street The Roots of Modern-day Pentecost* by Frank Bartleman, Bridge Publishing, 1980, page xviii.   8. Ibid, pages 56-57.
9. www.azusastreet100.net/history.htm#.
10. *Another Wave of Revival* by Frank Bartleman, 1962, 1982, Whitaker House, pages 73-74.   11. Ibid, pages 76, 93-94 and 97.
12. *The Apostolic Faith – Original Azusa Street Editions 1-13* on CDR, Azusa paper Number 1, page 4.
13. *Another Wave of Revival* by Frank Bartleman, 1962, 1982, pp.121-122 & 130.

Pyongyang Great Revival 1907-1910

1. Rev. Robert Thomas Jermain & North Korea - www.byfaith.co.uk/paulkorea.htm.
2. *Korean Church and Christian Book, History of the Korean Church and Review of 95 Different Christian Books, 2005 Frankfurter Buchmesses* (Frankfurt Book Fair), Christian Council of Korea, (CCK) 2005.

3. *Missions their Rise and Development* by Mrs Louise Creigton, Wiliams & Norgate, undated c.1912, page 87.
4. www.sarang.org - video presentation.
5. www.english.sarang.org/again_1907.asp.
6. *The Korean Pentecost & The Sufferings Which Followed* by William Blair and Bruce Hunt, The Banner of Truth Trust, (TBOTT), 1977, pages 52 and 61-66.
7. *When the Spirit's Fire Swept Korea* by Jonathan Goforth, Zondervan Publishing House 1943, Timothy Conjurske 1994, pages 7 and 16.
8. *The Korean Pentecost & The Sufferings Which Followed* by William Blair and Bruce Hunt, The Banner of Truth Trust, 1977, pages 67-72.
9. *When the Spirit's Fire Swept Korea* by Jonathan Goforth, Zondervan Publishing House 1943, Timothy Conjurske, 1994, page 9.
10. *The Korean Pentecost & The Sufferings Which Followed* by William Blair and Bruce Hunt, The Banner of Truth Trust, 1977, pages 72-74.
11. *When the Spirit's Fire Swept Korea* by Jonathan Goforth, Zondervan Publishing House 1943, Timothy Conjurske 1994, pages 17-21.
12. www.sarang.org - video presentation.
13. Ibid.
14. *When the Spirit's Fire Swept Korea* by Jonathan Goforth, Zondervan Publishing House 1943, Timothy Conjurske 1994, page 12.
15. *Goforth of China* by Rosalind Goforth, Zondervan Publishing House, 1937, pages 22-23.
16. *When the Spirit's Fire Swept Korea* by Jonathan Goforth, 1943, Timothy Conjurske, 1994, pages 12-14 and *The Korean Pentecost & The Sufferings Which Followed* by William Blair and Bruce Hunt, (TBOTT), 1977, page 82 – photo.
17. *When the Spirit's Fire Swept Korea* by Jonathan Goforth, Zondervan Publishing House 1943, Timothy Conjurske, 1994, pages 12-13.
18. *Charles M. Alexander – A Romance of Song and Soul-Winning* by Helen C. Alexander and J. Kennedy MacLean, Marshall Brothers Ltd, 1920, pp.163 and 167.
19. *The Bible in the World, Volume VII 1911*, British and Foreign Bible Society, (BAFBS) 1911, pages 26, 134 and 278.
20. *Missions their Rise and Development* by Mrs Louise Creigton, Williams & Norgate, undated c.1912, page 87.   21. Ibid, pages 201-203.
22. *The Korean Pentecost & The Sufferings Which Followed* by William Blair and Bruce Hunt, The Banner of Truth Trust, 1977, page 45 and *Korean Church and Christian Book - 2005 Frankfurter Buchmesses*, CCK, 2005, page 28.
23. *The Bible in the World, Volume VII 1911*, (BAFBS), 1911, pages 209-210.
24. *Missionary Joys in Japan* by Paget Wilkes, Morgan & Scott, 1913 page 143.
25. Ibid, pages 128-130.
26. Ibid, pages 128-130 and 137.
27. www.openheaven.com/forums.

Rusitu Revival 1915-1920

1. *Rees Howells Intercessor* by Norman Grubb, Lutterworth Press, 1952, pages 13-14, 17-18, 23 and 37.
2. Ibid, pages 130, 144, 146 and 153 and www.ReesHowells.co.uk.
3. *Thanksgiving Service: Life and Service of Rev. Samuel Rees Howells* 1912-2004.
4. *Thirsting For God* by Eva Stuart Watt, Marshall, Morgan & Scott, 1936 page 156.
5. *The Intercessions of Rees Howells* by Doris M. Ruscoe, The Lutterworth Press, 1983, 1991, pages 94-95.
6. *Rees Howells Intercessor* - Norman Grubb, Lutterworth Press, 1952, pp.160-161.
7. Ibid, pages 162-165 and 170.
8. *Evangelical Awakenings in Africa* - Edwin Orr, Bethany Fellowship, 1975, p.138.
9. *Rees Howells Intercessor* - Norman Grubb, 1952, pages 166, 172-174 and 179.
10. *Tales of an African Intercessor* by Michael Howard, Out of Africa Publishers, 1998, pages 51-52.

Budapest, Hungary 1937-1938
1. *Always Abounding, An Intimate Sketch of Oswald J. Smith of Toronto* by J. Edwin Orr, Marshall, Morgan & Scott, LTD., 1940, 1948 edition, page 74.
2. *Ireland Awakening* by Eva Stuart Watt, Moody Press, 1952, page17.
3. *Dynamite in Europe* by Eva Stuart Watt, Marshall, Morgan & Scott, 1939, chapter one.   4. Ibid, pages 143 and 145.   5. Ibid, pages 50-55.
6. *Ireland Awakening* by Eva Stuart Watt, Moody Press, 1952, page 17.
7. *Dynamite in Europe* by Eva Stuart Watt, Marshall, Morgan & Scott, 1939, pages 55-56.

Congo Revival 1953-1957
1. The missionary's letters were published in: *This is That*, Christian Literature Crusade (1954) and republished under the same title by Out of Africa Publishers (1997). WEC republished under the title *The Spirit of Revival* edited by Norman Grubb (2000) whilst chapter 27 of *The Liberating Secret* by Norman Grubb (1955) also covers the revival.
2. *Revival An Enquiry* by Max Warren, SCM Press LTD, 1954, page 38.
3. *This is That*, Out of Africa Publisher, (USA) undated, c.1997, page 9.
4. *The Spirit of Revival A first hand account of the Congo Revival of the 1950s* edited by Norman Grubb, Christian Focus Publications, (CFP) 2000, page 125.
5. Service of *Thanksgiving for the Life of Rev. David Morgan Davies* Nov. 2008.
6 *The Liberating Secret* by Norman Grubb, 1955, Lutterworth Press, pp.172-175.
7. *Floods On Dry Grounds* by Eva Stuart Watt, Marshall, Morgan & Scott, 1943.
8. *The Spirit of Revival* - Norman Grubb, (CFP), 2000, pages 79-81.
9. *This Is That*, Out of Africa Publishers, 1997, pages 64-65.
10. *The Spirit of Revival* - Norman Grubb, (CFP), 2000, page 125.
11. *This Is That*, Out of Africa Publishers, 1997, page 13.
12. Ibid, pages 13 and 15. 13. Ibid, pages 28, 31-32 and 34. 14. Ibid, pages 22-24.
15. Ibid, pages 60-61.   16. Ibid, pages 45, 47-49, 62, 67 and 69.
17. The Rev. David Davies died on the 16 November 2008, aged 98 years.

North Uist Revival 1957-1958
1. *Hebridean Journey* by Halliday Sutherland, 1940, The Catholic Book Club, p.176.
2. *When God Came Down an account of the North Uist Revival 1957-58* edited by John Ferguson, 2000, Lewis Recordings, pp.30-31 & 33.
3. *God's Answer, Revival Sermons* - Duncan Campbell, Faith Mission, 1960, p.92.
4. *Hearken O Daughter!* - Mary Morrison, Prairie Bible Institute, 1966, page 67.
5. *Hearken O Daughter!* - Mary Morrison, Prairie Bible Institute, 1966, page 69.
6. Some of these facts were from a Gaelic produced TV programme (which I watched whilst in North Uist) where Mary (nee Morrison) Peckham related the facts. I am unable to recollect the name of the TV programme.
7. *Hearken O Daughter!* - Mary Morrison, Prairie Bible Institute, 1966, page 70.
8. *When God Came Down an account of the North Uist Revival 1957-58* edited by John Ferguson, 2000, Lewis Recordings, pp.44-45 & 53.
9. Ibid, pp.46, 48, 50-52 & 53.
10. *Hearken O Daughter!* - Mary Morrison, Prairie Bible Institute, 1966, page 72-73.
11. *When God Came Down an account of the North Uist Revival 1957-58* edited by John Ferguson, 2000, Lewis Recordings, p.59. A special thank you to John Ferguson for allowing me to quote from his book.

Indonesian Revival 1964-1974
1. *The Revival in Indonesia* by Kurt Koch, Evangelization Publishers, West Germany, undated, 1970, pages 266-269.   2. Ibid, pages 102-103.
3. *The Ten Greatest Revivals Ever* by Elmer Towns and Douglas Porter, Servant Publications, 2000, page 171.
4. *The Revival in Indonesia* by Kurt Koch, Evangelization Publishers, 1970, p.159.

5. *The Ten Greatest Revivals Ever* by Elmer Towns and Douglas Porter, Servant Publications, 2000, page 171.
6. *The Revival in Indonesia* by Kurt Koch, Evangelization Publishers, pp.121-124 and *The Ten Greatest Revivals Ever* by Elmer Towns and Douglas Porter, p.171.
7. *The Gentle Breeze of Jesus* by Mel and Nona Tari, Creation House, 1974, pages 11 and 15.
8. *Like a Mighty Wind* by Mel Tari as told by Cliff Dudley, Kingsway Publications, 1971, 1978, pages 23-29.
9. *Nine O'Clock in the Morning* by Dennis J. Bennett, Logos International, 1970, page 196.
10. *Like a Mighty Wind* by Mel Tari - Kingsway Publications, 1971, 1978, pp.31-33.
11. Ibid, pages 79-80.   12. Ibid, pages 37-40.   13. Ibid, page 44.
14. *The Revival in Indonesia* by Kurt Koch, Evangelization Publishers, page 259.
15. *Like a Mighty Wind* by Mel Tari - Kingsway Publications, 1971, 1978, page 56.
16. *My Calvary Road* by Roy Hession, Lakeland/Marshall, Morgan & Scott, 1978, 1983, pages 243-245.
17. *The Gentle Breeze of Jesus* by Mel and Nona Tari, Creation House, 1974, pages 25-26.
18. See *Understanding Revival and Addressing the Issues it Provokes* by Mathew Backholer, ByFaith Media, 2009, pages 98 and 123-125.

Argentinean Revival 1982-1997
1. See *Revival Fires and Awakenings – Thirty-Six Visitations of the Holy Spirit* by Mathew Backholer, ByFaith Media, 2009, pages 105-107.
2. www.jesus.org.uk/ja/mag_talkingto_silvoso.shtml.
3. *Tales Of An African Intercessor* by Michael Howard, Out Of Africa Publishers, 1998, excerpts from chapter fourteen.
4. *Holy Spirit, I Hunger For You* by Claudio Freidzon, Creation House, 1997, p.45.
5. *The Rising Revival Firsthand Accounts of the Incredible Argentine Revival – And How It Can Spread Throughout The World* edited by C. Peter Wagner and Pablo Deiros, Renew Books, 1998, page 63.
6. *Holy Spirit, I Hunger For You* by Claudio Freidzon, Creation House, 1997, p.45.
7. www.jesus.org.uk/ja/mag_talkingto_silvoso.shtml.
8. *The Rising Revival* - C. Peter Wagner & Pablo Deiros, Renew Books, 1998, p.64.
9. *Holy Spirit, I Hunger For You* by Claudio Freidzon, Creation House, 1997, pages 59 and 63-65.
10. *The Rising Revival Firsthand* edited by C. Peter Wagner and Pablo Deiros, Renew Books, 1998, pages 99-100.   11. Ibid, excerpts chapter ten.
12. *Cross Pollination - The Miracle of Unity in Intercession, Revival and the Harvest* by Lila Terhune, Revival Press, imprint of Destiny Image, 1999, page 113.

Brownsville Revival 1995-2000
1. The majority of the quotes from Dr. Michael Brown were from *Revival – Not An Option*, teaching tape, 1997.
2. *Revival in Brownsville* by Steve Rabey, Thomas Nelson Publishers, 1998, p.4.
3. *Portal in Pensacola – The Real Thing Hits Brownsville* by Renee DeLories, Revival Press, 1997, page 128.
4. *Cross Pollination, The Miracle of Unity in Intercession, Revival & the Harvest* by Lila Terhune, Revival Press, imprint of Destiny Image, 1998, page ix.
5. *Children of Revival – Letting the Little Ones Lead* by Vann Lane, Destiny Image, 1998, pages 81-82.
6. *Revival in Brownsville* by Steve Rabey, Thomas Nelson Publishers, 1998, pages 76 and 211.   7. Ibid, page 160.
8. *Where Lions Feed*, - Rev. John Kilpatrick, teaching tape - Brownsville A0G, 1996.
9. *Portal in Pensacola – The Real Thing Hits Brownsville* by Renee DeLories, Revival Press, 1997, pages 158 and 162.

Shillong Revival 2006-2007
1. CWR PrayerTrack Oct-Dec -2006.
2. www.shillong.com.
3. http://torestoration.googlepages.com/howitallstarted.htm.
4-8. www.shillongrevival.com.
9. A special thank you to Barkos Warjri. Revised & updated Nov. 2007 & Dec. 2009.

Appendix A and B
1. *Revival and the Great Commission* by Mathew Backholer, ByFaith Media, 2007, page 68. 2. Ibid, page 36. 3. Ibid, page 68. *Global Revival* – 2010 edition.
4. *From Japan to Jerusalem* by Bishop E. Graham Ingham. Church Missionary Society, 1911, p.56.
5. www.pust.kr.

Other Books by Mathew Backholer

- *Revival Fires and Awakenings – Thirty-Six Visitations of the Holy Spirit, A Call to Holiness, Prayer and Intercession for the Nations.*
- *Global Revival – Worldwide Outpourings, Forty-Three Visitations of the Holy Spirit – The Great Commission.*
- *Understanding Revival and Addressing the Issues it Provokes*; so that we can intelligently cooperate with the Holy Spirit during times of revivals and awakenings and not reject His workings due to religious affections, physical phenomena or manifestations and that we may be not be caught unaware of the tactics of the enemy.
- *How to Plan, Prepare and Successfully Complete Your Short-term Mission*
- *Mission Preparation Training*

www.ByFaith.co.uk
www.RevivalNow.co.uk
www.MissionsNow.co.uk
www.GloryNow.co.uk - www.RevivalFire.co.uk
www.AwakeNow.co.uk - www.ReesHowells.co.uk
www.ProphecyNow.co.uk - www. ByFaithBooks.co.uk
www.ByFaithTV.co.uk - www. ByFaithDVDs.co.uk
www.ByFaithMedia.co.uk
www.UKPRAY.co.uk
www.GoPray.co.uk
www.xfaith.co.uk

Revival Fires and Awakenings – *Thirty-Six Visitations of the Holy Spirit, A Call to Holiness, Prayer and Intercession for the Nations* by Mathew Backholer. Whilst each revival is different, the author reveals the common characteristics and recurring experiences that come to the fore during four centuries of revivals and awakenings. Featuring 36 accounts of revivals in nineteen countries from six continents. 2009 edition – Twenty-two chapters.

Understanding Revival *and Addressing the Issues it Provokes* by Mathew Backholer. Revival is an amazing outpouring of the Holy Spirit but history records that many who have prayed for revival have rejected it when it came because they misunderstood the workings of the Holy Spirit and only wanted God to bless the Church on their terms. During times of heavenly visitations, there are Divine paradoxes and in the midst of God's dynamic, the devil will come to infiltrate and imitate so let us understand revival so that we do not reject it when He comes or bring the work of God into disrepute. 2009 edition – Thirty-one chapters.

Global Revival – *Worldwide Outpourings, Forty-Three Visitations of the Holy Spirit – The Great Commission* by Mathew Backholer. This book documents forty-three revivals from more than thirty countries on six continents. The author explores the Divine-human partnership of revival, explains how revivals are birthed and reveals the fascinating links between pioneering missionaries and the revivals that they saw in their fulfilment of the Great Commission. Learn from the past, be challenged for today and be inspired for the future! 2010 edition – Twenty-five chapters.

Great Christian Revivals on DVD is an inspirational and uplifting account of some of the greatest revivals in church history. Filmed on location in England, Wales and Scotland and drawing upon archive information, the stories of the Welsh Revival (1904-1905), the Hebridean Revival (1949-1952) and the Evangelical Revival (1739-1791) are brought to life in this moving documentary. Using computer animation, historic photos and depictions, the events of the past are weaved into the present, as the old and new are blended together to bring these stories to life. 2009 – 72 minutes.

How Christianity Made the Modern World by Paul Backholer. Christianity is the greatest reforming force that the world has ever known, yet its legacy is seldom comprehended. But now using personal observations from his research in over thirty-five nations, the author brings this legacy alive by revealing how Christianity helped create the path that led to Western liberty and laid the foundations of the modern world. 2009 – Thirty-seven chapters.

ByFaith – In Search of the Exodus on DVD. A three-thousand year old mystery will come alive as the epic tale of the biblical exodus will be tested and tried on the walls of Egyptian tombs and temples. Mathew and Paul Backholer search through ancient relics to find the evidence for the biblical exodus account. 2010.

The Exodus Evidence In Pictures - *The Bible's Exodus: The Hunt for Ancient Israel in Egypt, the Red Sea, the Exodus Route and Mount Sinai* by Paul Backholer. The search for archaeological data to validate the biblical account of Joseph, Moses and the Hebrew Exodus from ancient Egypt. 2010, 100+ colour photos.

ByFaith – World Mission DVD is a cutting edge and compelling reality TV documentary that shows the real experience of a backpacking style Christian short-term mission in Asia, Europe and North Africa. With no scripts, no safety net and no easy way out, Paul and Mathew Backholer shoot through fourteen nations, in an 85-minute real-life documentary, which was filmed over three years. *ByFaith – World Mission* is perfect for an evening of global adventure and is the very best of ByFaith TV – season one. 2008.

How to Plan, Prepare and Successfully Complete your Short-term Mission by Mathew Backholer is for volunteers, churches, independent STM teams and mission organisations. It is the ultimate guide to missions. For individuals, leaders, teams and those planning a Christian gap year – the why, where and when of STMs. From his many adventures in over thirty-five nations, Mathew reveals how to plan well, avoid the pitfalls and successfully complete your STM! Forty-eight Chapters 2010.

Mission Preparation Training by Mathew Backholer covers 29 topics in 35 lessons. The book will aid the reader to discern the voice of God, find His will and direction and how to implement and prepare for the call on their life as part of the Great Commission. Covering the various aspects and approaches which can be used in evangelism, practical discipleship and how Christians can enter into the fullness of God, by being set free and delivered from past bondages and afflictions; (in practical hands-on ministry) being made whole in body, soul and spirit, whilst being built up in the most holy faith. Also beneficial for everyday discipleship.

www.ByFaithBooks.co.uk – www.ByFaithDVDs.co.uk

Caracteristicas of Reavivamiento.

① Ambre por Dios
② Oracion.
③ Estudio Biblica — para estar Con Dios
④ Arrepentimiento/perdon
⑤